More praise for *Power Sales Writing*

For several years, we've provided the ladies and gentlemen of our sales teams with *Power Sales Writing* to help them write authentically and professionally. This updated version is even better!

Lucas McMaHill
Sr. Manager, Sales Incentives, Recognition, and Training
The Ritz-Carlton Hotel Company

It is more difficult every day to stand out amongst competitors, but with the style of communicating you'll learn from Sue, you'll win more business and make a stronger impact on your clients. This revised edition will *transform* the approach you use to write sales e-mails.

Gerilyn Horan
Director of Global Sales-North America
Langham Hospitality Group

In the competitive world of financial services, financial planners need an edge to impact potential clients and build strong client relationships. The communication techniques found in *Power Sales Writing* are essential tools to grow and develop a successful practice.

Daniel J. Young, CLU, ChFC, LLIF, CMP
Director of Event Planning and Recognition
Thrivent Financial for Lutherans

The revised version of *Power Sales Writing* provides even more practical tools and examples! It's exactly what sales professionals need to sell in today's dynamic marketplace.

Teri Jamison
General Sales Manager
Mid-Altantic Sales Office
Marriott International

POWER SALES WRITING

Using Communication to Turn Prospects into Clients

EXPANDED SECOND EDITION

SUE HERSHKOWITZ-COORE

New York Chicago San Francisco Lisbon London Madrid Mexico City
Milan New Delhi San Juan Seoul Singapore Sydney Toronto

The *McGraw·Hill* Companies

2 3 4 5 6 7 8 9 0 DOC/DOC 1 6 5 4 3 2 1

ISBN: 978-0-07-177014-9
MHID: 0-07-177014-3

e-ISBN   978-0-07-177080-4
e-MHID 0-07-177080-1

McGraw-Hill books are available at special quantity discounts to use as premiums and sales promotions or for use in corporate training programs. To contact a representative, please e-mail us at bulksales@mcgraw-hill.com.

This book is printed on acid-free paper.

In loving memory of my daddy, Philip Hershkowitz,
who would have liked this idea.

CONTENTS

ACKNOWLEDGMENTS

The first edition of *Power Sales Writing* came about because Larry Winget, then just a local speaker, told me that if I thought I had something to say, I was "stupid" not to say it. "Write a book," he said. Larry, it never would have happened without your less-than-gentle persuasion, and I am grateful for your wisdom.

Thank you also to Joe Charbonneau, my friend and mentor, who has since passed away, but will never leave my heart.

Thank you to all my clients over the years, who opened your "reader files" so that I could better understand why even with your awesome products and dedicated teams, the sales were slow to come.

Thank you to my workshop participants, who have been willing to let me tear apart their e-mails (with love) so that we could refocus the message to authentically gain the buyer's trust. Without reviewing your thousands of e-mails, I never would have known how challenging it can be for sales professionals to create messages that sell instead of just deliver information.

Thank you to Donya Dickerson, who agreed that there was a need to launch an update, and to all the editors at McGraw-Hill, who make sure that the message is easy to read and that I sound smart.

Thank you to my son, Michael, and to my mom and friends, who lately have seen me only through my Facebook posts and tweets.

And, thank you most of all to my husband, Bill, for always supporting me in everything I do and loving me even when I'm too busy to be particularly lovable. I love you.

INTRODUCTION

You had me at "hello."

—SPOKEN BY DOROTHY (RENÉE ZELLWEGER) IN *JERRY MAGUIRE*

D o your e-mails sell for you? Do they influence your prospect to take the next step? Do they advance the sale or the relationship? Do they create abundance for you? If you'd like to write e-mails that drive sales and convert leads, you've come to the right place.

The first edition of *Power Sales Writing* focused on creating written messages that connected with buyers. E-mail, however, was just taking over the world, smartphones didn't exist, and social media was little known in the world of business. This revised edition incorporates the realities of selling today, including the impact of responding on the go and how social media has influenced what people read and how they purchase.

When the primary—or only—way to communicate is through e-mail, the key to sales success is being able to write an e-mail that gets opened, read, and acted upon. Whether you're prospecting by e-mail, responding to an e-lead or e-mail request, or crafting a proposal or the transmittal message that goes with it, you will set yourself apart with the sales writing tips and strategic tools in this book.

Prospects and customers are just waiting for someone (you!) to sell to them in the way they want to buy. They're tired of receiving disingenuous e-mails that are irrelevant to them. They don't want to read about how you're writing "to introduce yourself" or because you want to "check in" or "touch base" with them. They are eager to be authentically engaged by (and give their business to) professionals who respect their time, pay attention to the details, and focus on their needs. You're about to see how this not only creates more sales, but makes writing easier than you ever imagined.

If you've ever sent a customer an e-mail you wish you hadn't, this book will save you from yourself! *Power Sales Writing* gives you the strategies you need to ensure that your ideas stand out. You'll discover fresh new ideas for differentiating your product or service and making it easy for your customer to buy from you. Whether your "competition" is sitting in the next cubicle, is a shiny new product down the road, or is a consistent set of hard-to-distinguish offerings, you can count on learning exciting methods to win the business and convert the leads.

This book offers you

- A treasure chest of templates to help you prospect with confidence—and drive business growth
- A simple, easy-to-implement procedure to make your point quickly, clearly, and concisely
- A process for applying tools of persuasion and influence in an authentic, customer-centric manner to make your messages pop

If you have always wanted to feel confident and comfortable with your writing skills, this book shows you exactly what to do. *Power Sales Writing* is packed with ideas to help you

- Write more quickly—up to 80 percent more quickly!
- Entice your prospect to read—and keep reading.
- Format your message for maximum impact.
- Advance the sale to the next step.

- Avoid embarrassing yourself with outdated, distracting expressions and words.
- Use your selling time more productively and profitably.
- Sound smarter and sell smarter than your competition.
- Extend your hand to engage buyers and make it easy for them to say yes.
- And much, much more!

With our current addiction to e-mail messaging, the ability to reach others through the written word has never been more important. Every idea, tool, and strategy in this book will help you become more effective and sell more, more easily. As in the movie *Jerry Maguire*, you'll have them at hello.

PART ONE

◆◆◆

GETTING STARTED

The scariest moment is always just before you start.

—STEPHEN KING

Results. Respect. Revenue.

That's what this book is about—writing in a way that gets you what you want by giving your reader what he needs.

When you use the techniques in this first section, you'll create winning sales messages quickly. You'll write e-mails that are more direct, more concise, and more persuasive. But wait, there's more! With the techniques you'll learn in this first part, not only will you write more efficiently, but you'll also be more effective. When you hit that Send button, you'll know that you've created an easy path for your prospect to follow, and you'll enjoy the confidence of knowing that both your intent and your content will be understood and appreciated.

Start now!

CHAPTER 1

◆ ◆ ◆

GETTING STARTED

*Organizing is what you do before you do something, so
that when you do it, it is not all mixed up.*

—A.A. MILNE, *WINNIE-THE-POOH*

I hate busywork. Drying dishes, for instance, is busywork. Why waste time drying dishes when the air will dry them? I could be accomplishing a million other things instead of just standing there, drying.

"Sharing ideas" at a workshop is another example of busywork that drives me nuts. When there is one right answer, don't make me waste time guessing what that answer is and discussing all the wrong ones. Just tell me the right answer and help me apply it.

Anything that doesn't help me move forward and get the job done, in my opinion, is busywork and should be eliminated. You can imagine my surprise, then, after despising being made to "outline" in school (busywork—why can't I just write the report?), when I realized that taking the time to organize my thoughts before writing (not to be confused with outlining!) would actually *propel* me forward and help to accomplish the job more quickly.

Here's what I learned: by taking the time to focus on your sales strategy and write your goals *before* you write your e-mail, you *save* time! "Measure twice, cut once." It applies to e-mail writing too.

◆◆◆

By taking the time to think through what you want your e-mail to accomplish before you start writing, you can save up to 80 percent of the time you spend writing.

THE LIFE-CHANGING AND VERY COOL THREE-STEP WRITING PROCESS

The three-step process you're about to read about will change your life. Seriously. Not only will you save time (a CEO I worked with claimed that it had taken him as long as "2½ hours to get started" until he learned this process), but the e-mails you write will be more concise, more persuasive, and more likely to get read. And there's more. You'll save additional time because your prospects will understand your intent and content the first time. They'll have fewer questions for you, and those outrageously annoying time-sucking back-forth-back-forth e-mails will be eliminated. By knowing what you want to achieve and what matters to your buyer, you'll present yourself as an organized, smart sales professional, and that is, as they say, "priceless."

What are the three steps?

- Plan it.
- Do it.
- Check it.

Planning your sales purpose before you write enables you to focus both on your sales goal (the outcome you'd like your e-mail to achieve) and the strategy to use to achieve that result. (Contrary to what many professionals think, the goal of an e-mail is rarely to close the business. Most selling messages are written to excite the buyer and earn the right to advance.) With a plan firmly in place, you write more quickly, more cleverly, and more successfully, and your clarity of purpose makes it much easier for your customer to say yes to you instead of to your competition.

PLANNING IS THE CATALYST FOR QUICK, CLEAR WRITING

Organizing before you write is the basis for clear, persuasive writing. All it takes is answering five questions. (With practice, you'll be able to do this in just a few seconds.) The questions act as a guide to help you focus on the specific outcome you'd like your e-mail to deliver, and the answers provide a clear path to successful writing and profitable selling. This planning, or "prewriting," step changes everything about the way you present your message, engage your buyer, and stand out from the crowd of competitors. Here are the five planning questions:

1. Why am I writing?
2. What do I want to say?
3. What do I want to accomplish?
4. What is the next step?
5. Have I provided a reason why this person would be delighted to do what I ask or say?

These (deceptively) simple questions will begin to transform the way you write. How?

Here is an example of a situation that screams for planning.

Situation: You're an experienced salesperson, but you're new with Company X. You need to start filling your sales funnel so that you can build business quickly. You're given a list of potential leads and know that you need to create a compelling e-mail to introduce yourself to these potential leads.

Without the prewriting step, you might create an e-mail similar to the one a workshop attendee submitted, prior to attending the training:

```
Hi Name,

Greetings from sunny Scottsdale!

I'm writing to introduce myself as your new sales
manager. I've recently taken over Sophie Spaniel's
position, and I'm excited about working with you.
My experience includes three years with a nonprofit
and most recently as a national sales manager for
a competitor, and I can say, I'm very glad to
be here!

Our hotel has undergone an $XX million renovation
in the last two years, and our ballroom space has
expanded to 15,000 square feet! The spa also was
enlarged, giving a total of 13,455 square feet of
serenity.

I'd love to invite you to come down to see us and
maybe have some lunch or a quick cup of coffee. It
would be fun to meet you in person! I look forward
to hearing from you soon.
```

Does this sound typical to you? Does it sound good? If you're wondering what is wrong with it or thinking, "That is exactly how I'd write it," your life is about to change. Just about *everything* is wrong with this sales message! If the writer had taken the time to thoughtfully plan her message, she would have realized that she shouldn't be writing to introduce herself, about the hotel features, or even about how much fun it would be to meet in person. We'll get to what she (and you) should be writing soon.

Planning Helps You Sell More Easily

Most salespeople are familiar with a sales goal planning process in which sales objectives are determined, then tracked and reviewed.

Knowing what they need to achieve to be successful (what their sales objectives are) guides their daily activities to ensure that those sales goals can be achieved (and exceeded).

Planning your e-mail messaging works similarly. An outcome is determined (for instance, you want your e-mail to persuade your prospect to accept your phone call next Tuesday), and that outcome guides how the e-mail is written. It's simple really. Knowing the purpose of your e-mail tells you what to leave in and what to leave out. Planning gives you a target to hit and eliminates wasted time and effort.

Answering the questions takes anywhere from 10 seconds to 2 minutes (none of which is busywork), but that time saves you time. The few seconds that you spend planning and organizing the sales strategy for your e-mail can save up to 80 percent of the time you currently spend writing (and rewriting and writing again).

♦♦♦

Determine the sales strategy so that your e-mail will sell more, more easily.

Put Your Plan in Print

It's important that you actually type or write the answers to the five questions rather than just think them through. There are several reasons for this:

1. **Interruptions happen.** Imagine that you're happily typing. You've thought through your purpose, and while it's fresh in your mind, you're writing and you're in the zone. Then the phone rings. Or your counterpart walks into your office. Or your dog nudges you, reminding you that it's time for her walk. When you try to direct your attention back to the sales message you were writing, your words have stopped flowing. Get-

ting back on track often involves frustration and a Starbucks. If you've written the answers to the five questions, however, a quick review of your answers is all you'll need, and you'll have that e-mail done in no time.

2. **No tricks**. The best thing you can do for yourself to improve both the effectiveness and the efficiency of your writing is to have a plan—and not a half-thought-out one. It's possible to pretend that you're thinking your message through when, in reality, you're splitting your mind (like when you're in a meeting but thinking about what you can say to escape the meeting). Take the time to type out the goal for your e-mail to eliminate the temptation to *not* focus on your message thoroughly and thoughtfully. Bring focus and clarity to your thoughts.

3. **New habits**. Developing any new habit takes discipline and time. It's human nature and oh-so-much-easier to fall back into more comfortable and convenient old patterns than to attempt something new. Just like skiing or playing golf, the more you do it, the better you get (well, maybe golf is a bad analogy). Make answering the five questions as routine as flossing.

4. **Time.** The two minutes you spend answering the questions saves many times that. You eliminate
   - The time-wasting write-delete-revise, write-delete-revise writing pattern
   - Staring at a blank screen, not knowing how to start
   - Starting your message with drivel (and possibly losing the opportunity to have your e-mail read)
   - Wasting time writing another message to clarify the message that you just sent
   - Sounding unprofessional and unprepared

Planning your message (prewriting) is smart because it prepares you to write more powerfully and more persuasively. You begin with a clear understanding of your message's purpose.

———————————————◆◆◆———————————————

Use your e-mail to achieve your goals. Set your target and take aim.

———————————————————————————————

Once you are clear about your writing sales strategy, it's easy to write to make the sale.

CHAPTER 2

◆ ◆ ◆

PLAN IT: SAVE UP TO 80 PERCENT OF WRITING TIME

Preparation is everything. Noah did not start building the ark when it was raining.

—WARREN BUFFETT

may have led you astray. The five questions you learned in the last chapter aren't exactly right. In practice, the questions are actually simpler and can be abbreviated to

1. Why?
2. What?
3. Accomplish?
4. Next step?
5. Delighter?

Before we get to the shorthand version, however, we'll need to expand the questions for full understanding and ease of application.

Looking at the prewriting questions, it would be easy to think that they focus on the writer. Additional verbiage clarifies the questions' intent.

The first question, "Why am I writing?" isn't so much about why *you* are writing, as the question seems to imply, but why you are writing *that will matter to the reader.* (Notice how the emphasis has changed.) The more your writing is framed in terms of the reader, the more likely your reader is to actually read the message (which, of course, is quite helpful).

By thinking about this first question from your customer's perspective—by, as much as possible, *becoming* your customer—you can move away from writing about your product and move toward writing about why or how your prospect might benefit from the product. Whether your prospect already knows that he needs your service or has no clue that it even exists, when you focus on solving challenges that he has and can make it clear that your intent is to help him create greater success, you're more likely to have the chance to start a meaningful sales conversation.

◆◆◆

Planning enables you to think through your sales strategy.

The second question, like the first, should also be about the reader. Thinking through your response from the prospect's perspective requires you to consider the difference between what you're selling (a drill bit) and what the prospect is buying (a hole). What do you want to say in your e-mail *that will matter to the reader?*

The answer to the second question is always an extension of the first.

Here is an example. Let's say you receive a request for information about availability of your E-mail Ninja Kit. Before writing back, you'll want to answer the five questions. If your answer to Question 1, "Why am I writing that will matter to my reader?" is, "To get her excited about how much time she can save with the new E-mail Ninja Kit," you're already an expert sales strategist. (Notice that the answer to the question isn't about the E-mail Ninja Kit; it's about how much time the prospect can save with the kit.) Align your response to Question 2, "What do I want to say that will matter to the reader?" with your first response; explain to her *how* she can save time with the kit. (Again, this isn't so much about the kit as it is about the specific benefit that she receives from the kit.)

◆ ◆ ◆

Planning your message from your reader's perspective is key.

It's not until the third question, "What do I want to accomplish?" that you get to think about what you, the writer, actually want. This is your chance to be self-focused. What is it that you want this e-mail to do for you? Be careful here, though. If you're going to become a sales writing expert, don't leap to what you'd ultimately like to accomplish: closed business, a sale, a contract—12 million E-mail Ninja Kits sold! For this planning question to give you an edge, think more precisely and locally: "What do *I* want to accomplish *in this specific e-mail?*" Do you want to start a trusting relationship, earn the right to submit a proposal, learn more so that you are able to prepare a proposal, persuade her to complete the order form you've attached, motivate her to call you, or influence her to accept your call? Think of the specific action you want as a result of sending this e-mail.

Now that you've determined what you want (Question 3), you get to ask for it in Question 4, "What is the next step in the buying process?" When you are answering the fourth question, the two most important considerations are

- Who will take the next step?
- What precisely will that next step be?

You'll want to make both those points crystal clear to your prospect, and that's hard to do if you, the writer, aren't clear about them to start with.

Often, the next step seems so obvious to the person who is writing that he forgets to include it. A nonprofit I worked with had this incredibly emotional letter about the dire straits of sick children. The "sales" message talked about the urgent need for donations and appealed to "prospects" to donate. Yet the organization never asked for what it wanted—money. It never defined the next step by including exactly what should happen after the reader finished reading. It missed a golden opportunity to increase its "sales" by not including something like, "Please write your check for $25, $100, $1,000, or whatever you can afford, and mail it today. Please don't delay. You have the power to help right this very moment." If you want something, ask for it!

Thinking again about the E-mail Ninja Kits you're selling, if you respond to the lead request you received ("Do you have information on your E-mail Ninja Kits, and are they currently available?") with only, "Yes, we have the E-mail Ninja Kits available for shipment, and I've attached the information you requested," but what you really want (Question 3) is for the person to complete the form you've attached and e-mail it back to you, you've neglected to make that next step clear. It may be implied, particularly if you add, "I've attached an order form for you," but like the nonprofit, why simply imply when you can increase sales by clarifying exactly what the next step is? In this case, the next step that makes the most sense is to ask the prospect to take the action: "I've attached a price list and an easy-to-complete order form for your convenience. Please e-mail or fax (555-555-5555) your completed form today. As soon as I receive the number of kits you would like, we will ship them immediately."

◆◆◆

Another way to look at Question 4 is: "What is the next step in the prospect's buying process?"

Question 5, "Have I provided a reason why this person would be delighted to do what I ask or say?" reminds the buyer that there is a payoff for him if he does, or accepts, the next step. It's the motivation to do what you are suggesting. Glenn Kreighbaum, a workshop participant, called Question 5 "the delighter," and I've adopted that phrase here.

This last question increases the worth of Question 4. It elevates the next step from being only an action step (do this now) to being a persuasive message (do this now so that you can enchant customers with your E-mail Ninja skills and grow more business). Question 5 transforms the self-focused answer to Question 3, "What do I want to accomplish in this specific e-mail?" into a customer-centric answer. Now you're asking, if I want to accomplish X, "Have I provided enough motivation for the prospect to accept or take that next step? The answer to Question 5 provides buying motivation. Have I provided a reason why the prospect would be delighted to do what I ask?" This follow-up question also gives you your perfect closing line.

What might motivate your E-mail Ninja Kit lead to complete the order form in a timely manner? Here are three possible benefits to your buyer:

- She'll start saving time immediately.
- She'll have more time to accomplish her other important tasks.
- She can start using the kit immediately to enchant prospects and grow business.

◆◆◆

Leave your reader with an emotion, not a procedure.

With a clear writing purpose in mind, the sales message to the E-mail Ninja Kit lead might sound like this:

```
Hi Name,

You've made a great choice considering the ABC E-mail
Ninja Kit! You'll save time, sound professional, and
get great results from all your e-mail messages.

E-mail Ninja Kits are still available for immediate
shipping. As you requested, I've attached additional
information. For your convenience, I've also included
an easy-to-complete order form. Please indicate how
many kits you would like, include your shipping
address and credit card information, and e-mail it
to me, or fax it to 555-555-5555. As soon as your
order is received, your kits will be shipped to you
```

```
so that you can start saving time, have more time to
accomplish your other important tasks, and enchant
your customers with your extraordinary writing and
customer service skills.
```

Depending on your personality and writing style, you might want to make this e-mail more concise and crisp. For now, however, please consider the differences between simply providing information (here it is; how many do you want?) and adding persuasion to the message (here is why you're smart for ordering this; how many do you want; you'll be delighted that you made this smart decision). This e-mail is geared to a prospect who may be shopping around (as many prospects do) and may need a bit of encouragement to make the purchase, and especially to feel safe and confident enough to purchase it from you. The planning questions are an ideal way to think through your strategy and write a complete, clear, customer-focused e-message that sells.

PUTTING PLANNING INTO PRACTICE

Here, then, are the complete planning questions:

1. Why am I writing (that will matter to the reader)?
2. What do I want to say (that will matter to the reader)?
3. What do I want to accomplish (in this specific e-mail)?
4. What is the next step (in the buying process)?
5. Have I provided a reason why this person would be delighted to do what I ask or say?

Remember the situation from the previous chapter in which you are new with Company X and you want to fill your sales funnel to build business quickly? Here is how the e-mail was written, without benefit of thinking through the writing or sales strategies that might influence the buyer:

Hi Name,

Greetings from sunny Scottsdale!

I'm writing to introduce myself as your new sales manager. I've recently taken over Sophie Spaniel's position, and I'm excited about working with you. My experience includes three years with a nonprofit and most recently as a national sales manager for a competitor, and I can say, I'm very glad to be here!

Our hotel has undergone an $XX million renovation in the last two years, and our ballroom space has expanded to 15,000 square feet! The spa also was enlarged, giving a total of 13,455 square feet of serenity.

I'd love to invite you to come down to see us and maybe have some lunch or a quick cup of coffee. It would be fun to meet you in person! I look forward to hearing from you soon.

When the five questions are applied, the e-mail's intent and focus change dramatically.

1. **Why am I writing that will matter to the reader?** Will your prospect care about *your* desires: that *you* want to introduce *yourself*? Will it matter to your prospect (at this point) if *you're* happy with *your* choice to work with this new company? Will it make one iota of difference to your prospect if *you* think it would be fun to meet him or what *you* are looking forward to?

   By answering *why am I writing* from the reader's (buyer's) perspective, it's easy to see that the original e-mail is on the wrong track. What appeared, without a clear plan, to be a simple message of introduction turns out to be something else entirely.

2. **What do I want to say that will matter to the reader?** Will the prospect care whether you have 13,455 square feet of spa space? Do you think he'll physically step it off to confirm what you said? Really? He may, indeed, be interested in knowing how many treatment rooms you have so that he'll know whether you can accommodate his group's needs, but what will he do knowing the actual footage? What can you say that will pertain to the reader?

   Remember that the answers to Questions 1 and 2 focus on your buyer. Do your best to become your customer. What matters to her about what you have to offer?

Think: customer, customer, me.

---

3. **What do I want to accomplish in this specific e-mail?** In this question, you finally get to consider your own objectives for the e-mail. Be careful to think in terms of small steps, though. If you want the prospect to see the hotel, what has to happen first? Think locally and specifically in this e-mail, rather than globally and generically. Will you need to phone the prospect to discuss a convenient time for him to visit the hotel? If so, then what you want to accomplish *in this e-mail* is to persuade him to take your call to set up the visit. That is the very next step in both the selling and the buying process. And, if you want the prospect to take your call, your e-mail has to pique his interest enough so that when he sees your name come up on his caller ID, he picks up the phone instead of letting you go to voice mail. Alternatively, maybe the action you want is to have him take the next step. If you want him to e-mail or call you with suggested times to visit, your e-mail must motivate him to do just that.

4. **What is the next step in the buying process?** This answer is easy and critical to success (but it was missing from the original e-mail). If what you want is for the prospect to take your call, then the next step is: "I'll call you Friday morning." If what you want to accomplish is for him to e-mail you back, the next step is: "Please e-mail me when it will be convenient for you to stop by for a site visit and . . ."

5. **Have I provided a reason why this person would be delighted to do what I ask or say?** This question takes us back to the reader's motivation. What's in it for him to come to see you? In the original introductory e-mail, the reason given was that it would be fun (for the salesperson), and a free lunch was also offered. At this point, because the prospect doesn't yet know how much fun you are, he probably won't be motivated by the fact that *you* will find it fun to meet *him*. Also, a free lunch may seem like a nice promotion, but in "becoming your customer," you see that most likely he can expense his lunches and is offered more free lunches than time to eat them. Having lunch with you isn't a compelling reason to visit the hotel. And, if he's motivated by the free lunch, you may be in trouble. If this prospect is coming only because he wants a free lunch, he may not be qualified.

Now it's your turn. Here are the questions again. The abbreviated questions follow, and we'll start using the shortened version in the next chapter.

1. Why am I writing that will matter to the reader? (Why?)
2. What do I want to say that will matter to the reader? (What?)
3. What do I want to accomplish in this specific e-mail? (Accomplish?)
4. What is the next step in the buying process? (Next step?)
5. Have I provided a reason why this person would be delighted to do what I ask? (Delighter?)

Using the scenario described, take a moment to write your answers. This is an "open-book test," so you may want to reread the hints provided earlier. Taking the time to write your responses will give you the practice you need to feel confident and competent using this prewriting skill. (Don't cheat yourself by just *thinking* about your answers!)

Because this is a new writing strategy, many people will be tempted to fall back into their old patterns and answer the questions this way:

1. *Why am I writing (that will matter to the reader)?* To introduce myself.
2. *What do I want to say (that will matter to the reader)?* Our hotel has undergone an exciting new $XX million renovation, and I'd like you to come for a site visit.
3. *What do I want to accomplish in this specific e-mail?* Book the business/get the prospect to do a site tour.
4. *What is the next step in the buying process?* The prospect contacts me so that we can meet.
5. *Have I provided a reason why this person would be delighted to do what I ask or say?* It will be fun, it's a free lunch, and she'll get to the see the exciting new changes in the hotel.

If you answered that way, you've fallen into the trap of thinking about your product before your customer. It's *me, me, customer* thinking instead of the more strategic *customer, customer, me.*

Sales professionals love their own products (and should!), which makes it easy to understand why they (you!) write about the product instead of about how the reader can benefit from the product. Another reason for self-centered writing is not thinking of e-mail writing as part of their sales strategy. Too often, people say to themselves, "I'll just send an e-mail." It's never *just* an e-mail! Use every communication, including every interaction through e-mail, to set yourself apart and sell more, more easily, by focusing on the customer's needs rather than on your own.

Let your competitors think, "It's just an e-mail." Outsmart them by using your e-mail sales messages to love your customer and sell more.

Let's go back to the scenario. Bravo if you answered the planning questions this way:

1. *Why am I writing that will matter to the reader?* To excite the prospect about how successful her next meeting can be at our remodeled hotel.
2. *What do I want to say that will matter to the reader?* Your attendees will stay focused and energized in our comfortable new space.
3. *What do I want to accomplish in this specific e-mail?* Pique her interest enough so that she'll take my phone call and we'll start a trusting relationship.
4. *What is the next step in the buying process?* I phone her Tuesday.
5. *Have I provided a reason why she would be delighted to do what I ask or say?* She can see for herself how comfortable and energized her attendees will be learning and networking in our perfect new space.

At this point, you might be thinking: "Wait, what about introducing myself? Don't I need to say who I am? Isn't that important in starting the relationship?"

I'll answer your question with my own: do you truly believe your reader can't figure out who you are from your e-mail signature line?

Until they know how much you care about them, they don't care about who you are or what you know.

It's true that there are some circumstances in which it may be important to tell your reader a bit about yourself. If you took over for Sophie Spaniel, especially if your prospect and Sophie had a great relationship, your prospect may wonder why she is hearing from you and not from Sophie. If this is the case, the purpose of your message will be different from what was previously suggested. In either case, your e-mail will still be about the prospect—and helping her feel comfortable and confident—and not about introducing yourself.

Here are the answers to the prewriting questions for this (new) scenario:

1. *Why am I writing that will matter to the reader?* To help the prospect feel confident and comfortable that her next meeting will be just as successful as the last (if not more successful), and that she can expect to experience a seamless transition between Sophie and me.

2. *What do I want to say that will matter to the reader?* She can count on the excellent service that she has received in the past and highly successful, productive meetings.

3. *What do I want to accomplish in this specific e-mail?* Build a trusting relationship so that she'll be willing to take my call and be happy to work with me and remain loyal to my company.

4. *What is the next step in the buying process?* I call her in two weeks.

5. *Have I provided a reason why she would be delighted to do what I ask or say?* We'll review her meeting objectives so she can feel comfortable and well taken care of.

In Chapter 2, you'll see the revision for this "introductory" e-mail. You'll see that it highlights what the reader can rely on, and benefit from, rather than who I am or what matters to me.

Knowing what you want to achieve, preparing your sales strategy, and planning your e-mail's purpose can change your writing, your sales success, and your life!

◆ ◆ ◆

Planning your sales writing purpose—knowing your intent and content—is the key to your writing success.

As you become more comfortable with this sales writing planning skill, not only will you find yourself creating more powerful sales e-mails more quickly, but you'll also find yourself selling more profitably and closing more business.

CHAPTER 3

◆ ◆ ◆

DO IT: WHY BEING CREATIVE IS LESS IMPORTANT THAN YOU THINK

The beautiful part of writing is that you don't have to get it right the first time, unlike, say, a brain surgeon.

—ROBERT CORMIER

Doing it is the second step in the three-step writing process. This is the easiest part because you already know what you want to say and what you need to achieve.

To get into a writing flow, picture yourself talking to your prospect instead of writing. With the answers to your planning questions in mind, what would you say to your prospect? Type your words, using a normal, conversational, comfortable style. Don't criticize yourself while you write, don't worry if you ramble, and don't be concerned if your punctuation is awful. During the next step, checking, you'll have time to make certain that the message rocks in every way. Right now all you need to do is get your message out of you and onto your screen. As you write, compare what you're saying with what you planned. Are you moving toward your goal?

Keep in mind that in your e-mail, you don't need to use the exact words you used to answer the planning questions. Neither do you need to write your message in the same order in which you answered the five questions. The answers are there guiding you to ensure that you hit your mark.

Whatever you do, avoid the "overthinking" trap. Overthinking during this step can cause great frustration. All you're doing is creating a sales message based on the outcome you've planned. In Step 1, planning, you analyzed your outcome and clarified your sales strategy. Now simply allow yourself to "talk" your message through your fingers. Go for it! You can (and will) check and edit later. Right now, you are expressing your point easily, effortlessly, and efficiently. You're creating a message that is aligned with your goals.

You may be thinking that this flow of ideas happens only to people who "know how to write." Yes, and that would be you. This isn't about writing the Great American Novel. It's about writing a business message that engages your customer, and you do that successfully every day in conversations at meetings, over lunch, and on the phone. Knowing how to write for today's business world requires that you know how to communicate in an authentic, relevant, and transparent manner. Planning your message and being focused on your customer helps you to do that.

If, however, you have negative self-talk going on about your writing skills, it's likely that you're listening to the critical little voice (the left hemisphere of your brain) reminding you of former bad writing experiences and keeping you from doing your best work.

Our brains are divided into two hemispheres: the creative portion creates, and the analytical part (you guessed it) offers analytical and critical thought. Because writing—the flowing of the words—is a creative step, we needn't involve that critical part during the creative writing phase. (The analytical part was engaged in the planning process and will once again be called upon during the next step.)

Ignore all analytical whispers ("That doesn't sound right." "You can't do this." "You're a salesperson, not a writer." "Remember that awful paper you wrote in the seventh grade? This sounds worse." "Stop writing. Check your e-mail. Write a tweet. Check the ball scores." "You're a loser."). You can easily quiet your analytical brain by reminding yourself that you'll get the opportunity to criticize yourself—to review and revise—before you hit Send. But not now. Now, you're creating your message just as if you were talking to your prospect.

Here's another tip: if you can't think of the exact word you'd like to use, just keep going. Instead of stopping the creative flow to analyze word choices (or beat yourself up), simply type the word WORD or use a line of dashes or a jumble of numbers or symbols (994372 or &^%$#*) to indicate a place that you'll come back to during the check step. Allow yourself only to create during the creative step.

◆◆◆

Writing is a three-step process. (1) Planning is an analytical step. (2) Writing is creative. (3) Checking is analytical.

Keep moving forward with your words, no matter what. Your message doesn't need to be perfect yet because there is a prewired opportunity to make it better. (This is why I love writing. We have the wonderful opportunity to revise and improve everything. When we speak, we don't have that luxury. Our listener hears, in real time, the sometimes incoherent or poorly chosen words that spew from our mouths. There is nothing we can do—other than try to extricate foot from mouth! When we write, we get to extricate before the reader even sees our foot. Sweet.)

DO IT

How would you "do" the situation from Chapter 1? The writer's initial goal was to write an e-mail of introduction. When we applied the planning questions, it became evident that the point of the sales message—the sales strategy—should be something other than to talk about what matters to the writer. To review, here are the answers to the planning questions for that first situation:

1. *Why am I writing that will matter to the reader?* To excite the prospect about how successful her next meeting can be at our remodeled hotel.
2. *What do I want to say that will matter to the reader?* Your attendees will stay focused and energized in our comfortable new space.
3. *What do I want to accomplish in this specific e-mail?* Pique her interest enough so that she'll take my phone call and start a trusting relationship.
4. *What is the next step in the buying process?* I phone her Tuesday.
5. *Have I provided a reason why she would be delighted to do what I ask or say?* She can see for herself how comfortable and energized her attendees will be learning and networking in our perfect new space.

Here is your opportunity to do it. Knowing what needs to be accomplished, "talk" out your words. Live Nike's slogan and "Just do it!" If you were talking to that prospect instead of writing, what would you say?

You might write something like this:

```
Hi Name,

Your next meeting will be even more exciting at our
newly renovated hotel. Wait until you see the changes
since you were here last. Your attendees will definitely
stay focused and energized in our comfortable new space.

I'm hopeful that I've piqued your interest enough
that you'd like to visit us to see what your
attendees will experience.
```

Even without the third step (your opportunity to check and revise, tweak, and improve), would you agree this e-mail is a stronger, more persuasive sales message than the original? Do you agree that the writer has a better chance of achieving his sales goals?

It's a more persuasive sales message because it

- Focuses on the reader
- Excludes all the stuff that the reader isn't interested in (and won't read anyway)
- Is truthful
- Is specific
- Is clear
- Is exciting

Is this e-mail the best e-mail on the planet? No. No problem. (You can probably see some glaring omissions already.) We have one more step to ensure that we write the most effective e-mail, and we'll get to that in the next chapter. Notice, however, that this sales letter is stronger and more reader-focused because of the two minutes (or less) spent planning.

◆◆◆

It's not "just" an e-mail; it's an e-mail designed to achieve results.

Here is another situation to help you apply Steps 1 and 2:

This morning at 6:00 a.m., a prospect that you met at a trade show last week calls you on your mobile. She says she is very sorry to bother you at such an early hour, but she learned late last night that she had to fly to London today, and she is leaving immediately. She is calling you to see whether, based on the quick conversation at your trade show booth last week, you can do X for her. You have no idea whether you can do X. It's 6:00 a.m., she woke you up, and your laptop is in your home office down the hallway, past the bedrooms of your two sleeping children and your dog. Before you can commit to fulfilling her request, you have to check the delivery calendar, and you don't have access to it at the moment. You (groggily) tell her this, but you can hear the airplane announcement in the background telling her and the other passengers that they must shut down all mobile devices. She has no time to wait on the phone and asks again if you think you can do X. "I'll try," you say. You hear her exhale as she says, "Oh, thank you *so* much. I have to go."

You hang up the phone, and you know that she heard "I'll try" as "Yes!" (even though you never said that). You're fully awake now, so you put on your robe and slippers and tiptoe down the hall, with your now excited dog panting at your side. You turn on the lights of your office and see that there is no way—no possibility—that you can do what she has asked. You tie your robe around your waist, let the dog out, pray that the children stay asleep, and sit down to write an e-mail to her, hopeful that her plane has WiFi service and that she is using it. If not, your e-mail will be waiting for her when she lands at Heathrow airport.

What will your e-mail say? Without analyzing your intent, you might write something like this (after all, you haven't had even one cup of coffee and the kids will be awake soon):

```
Hi BC,

Hope your trip was good. I checked, and there is no
way I can get X done this week. I'm sorry.
```

Admittedly, this response was quick and easy to write. But was it effective? Will you get the result you want from this e-mail? Instead of writing without thinking (never a good policy), plan your message. Write your answers to the five organizational questions, here in their abbreviated form:

1. Why?
2. What?
3. Accomplish? (This can be further shortened to Acc?)
4. Next step? [You may want to shorten this to Next? or Act? (for Action needed).]
5. Delighter?

Here are my answers:

1. *Why?* To provide a solution to her request.
2. *What?* Here are three possible solutions: A, B, and C.
3. *Accomplish?* Build a trusting relationship; Motivate her to follow up with me
4. *Next step?* She e-mails me to tell me which option is best for her.
5. *Delighter?* She can count on me to follow through as soon as I receive her decision.

You may have a different purpose for writing and a different set of answers. (There is always more than one right answer.) As long as you are clear in your purpose, you'll write an e-mail that is persuasive, professional, and productive.

You've completed the first step of the three-step writing process. Now, without overthinking, picture the prospect. What would you say to her? Write what you would say, knowing that you will be able to come back to your draft to perfect it.

Here is one possibility:

```
Hi BC,

Hope your trip was great, and I have to admit to
being a bit jealous! London! How cool is that?! I've
always wanted to shop in those boutiques on Bond
Street (though I doubt I can afford them).

I appreciate your thinking of me to do X for you.
Here are the alternatives that might work for you:

A . . .

B . . .

C, your requested option, can't be accomplished
until September 9, and I know that is about 9 days
too late for you. We also might be able to expedite
```

```
shipment for you at an additional cost of $$$. I'll
need to check further on this if this is an option
you wish to pursue.

What will work best? Please let me know which option
is best for you, or if you have another idea, and
I'll follow through as soon as I receive your e-mail.
Please let me know.
```

◆◆◆

The good part about writing is that you get a second chance—a chance to proof what you wrote and, if necessary, take your foot out of your mouth.

This e-mail is *way* too wordy, but it is clearly aligned with the planning goals. Even as wordy as it is here, you'll be much more successful sending this message than the blunt option that we looked at earlier in this chapter. (We'll make the revision more concise soon.)

The great news is that once you create your message, you get to review and improve it. Rather than trying for perfection with your first draft, you'll save time and effort by *not* analyzing while you're creating and thus splitting your brain's focus. Count on making changes later. Give yourself the latitude and freedom to create a message that is based on your planning. Feel the flow. You're on your way to building a meaningful and trusting relationship with this client.

USE YOUR SALES WRITING STRATEGY TO MAKE SELLING EASY

Read this actual sales letter (city and Web site changed to protect the guilty) and decide for yourself whether the writer accomplished anything.

Dear Name,

Pupsville is rapidly becoming a premier golf destination in the United States. Our perfect climate and abundance of golf courses make year-round golf available for both you and your meeting attendees. In order to help you think about Pupsville when you think about golf, we've enclosed a special gift and an opportunity to qualify for an additional bonus.

As a fellow golfer, we're sure you appreciate the value of an established handicap. Enclosed please find a complimentary one-year membership to golf-r-usworld. com (a $24.00 value). Log onto the Web site and enter your password to begin your journey through the various offerings, including a course locator, golfing games, and the opportunity to establish a handicap by posting your individual scores.

If you respond by e-mail, we'll personally send you a sleeve of Pupsville-grown XYZ free-range golf balls. *High-scoring PGA golfer name here* and many other PGA tour professionals have trained these special balls. They're straight from this year's PGA tour at Champion National, and we invite you to take them out for a drive.

Our thanks in advance to you. We're looking forward to your response.

Sincerely,

Your Sales Representative

This e-mail *appears* to be well written; the salesperson selected nice words and adhered to the rules of grammar (for the most part). But if the intention of this e-mail is to help the salesperson sell, it failed miserably. The only outcomes that this sales rep can expect are to give away lots of golf balls and magazine subscriptions and fool herself into thinking that she is moving closer to meeting her sales quota.

What was she thinking? She was thinking that by providing her prospect with information and bribing him with free balls and a magazine, she'd get a response. I'm betting that she would say that her e-mail focused on her prospect, but would you agree? (Say no, please!) She could have created a customer-centric, persuasive sales message, one that would help her get the result and revenue that she wants, if instead of using the "let's-throw-it-all-against-the-wall-and-hope-something-sticks" theory, she had used the three-step writing process.

Here is what I think the writer was attempting to accomplish by writing this e-mail:

1. *Why?* To create excitement about the prospect's highly successful golf events and meetings in Pupsville.
2. *What?* You can expect great attendance when you schedule a meeting in Pupsville. Attendees love coming here!
3. *Accomplish?* To pique the prospect's interest so that he will either (decide which of these you want before writing)
   a. Accept a call
   b. Respond to the e-mail
   c. Click on a link for more info
4. *Next step?* I call him Thursday.
5. *Delighter?* He can drive attendance to his next association meeting and get a sleeve of cool golf balls, too.

Thoughtful planning will prevent the writer from giving away freebies (*complimentary one-year membership to golf-r-usworld.com and . . . If you respond by e-mail, we'll personally send you a sleeve of Pupsville-grown XYZ free-range golf balls*) to every Tom, Dick, and Harriet! It will also help the sales representative sell more successfully.

With the prewriting answers in mind, how would you "do" this message? One way to make the creative step easy is to imagine yourself at a networking event. You've struck up a conversation with the person sitting next to you—a hot prospect!—and he says to you, "So tell me, why I should schedule my next meeting in Pupsville?" What would you say?

You might say something like this:

```
Thanks for asking! Meeting attendance is always huge
when meetings are in Pupsville. It's amazing how
when attendees and guests find out the meeting is in
Pupsville, with the amazing variety of things to do,
the fresh air away from the city traffic and smog, and
the fabulous, world-renowned golf, programs double
in size, to the delight of the association! The other
thing is that there is an abundance of unique learning
environments, everything Green certified to save the
planet, of course, to help attendees feel good and stay
focused on getting their work accomplished. I see so
many attendees get off the shuttle when they arrive from
the airport, and they don't look very happy. By the time
they leave, they're energized and ready to be productive
again. Would you like to come visit? You'll see how much
your members will love meeting in Pupsville!
```

Start with Hi and sign your name to this conversation, and you have a pretty decent e-mail! The planning goal, to pique the prospect's interest in his success, was accomplished. We'll make changes in the third step, but, again, the differences between the original e-mail and this conversational version are dramatic.

With this sales message, the rep excites the prospect about possibilities that are meaningful to the prospect and his attendees. The sales professional no longer has to give away the store. She moves toward her goal with less effort—and much less expense, both in promotional "giveaway" gifts and in the time spent chasing unqualified leads (people who just want that sleeve of golf balls). (You can still give gifts, but you get to surprise and delight qualified prospects with your generosity rather than use the gifts as bait.)

◆◆◆

Once you know what you need to achieve, do it! Talk out your message. Allow yourself to create without self-critique.

Powerful, coherent, results-oriented writing starts first with planning and moves to doing. You plan to determine your purpose, and then you write to get the message out of you and onto the screen. The next chapter is like the icing on the cake. It's the final step that ensures that your writing is concise, clear, crisp, and customer-focused; it's your opportunity to ensure that you represent yourself, your organization, and your brand professionally, persuasively, and profitably.

CHAPTER 4

◆ ◆ ◆

CHECK IT: THE FAILURE-PROOF STEP

To write is human, to edit is divine.

—STEPHEN KING, *ON WRITING*

You've finished the hard and easy parts! Yay! You took the time to analyze why you're writing (hard because for most salespeople you just want to go full steam ahead and start writing right away), and you "talked out" your words onto your screen (the easy part, because you have a clear and certain outcome in mind). Another minute or two and you'll be ready to hit that Send button, confident that your reader will understand both your message and your intent. Ignore this crucial last step, however, and you risk losing the possibility of a sale, not to mention your professional reputation.

Here is an example of what I mean. This is an actual follow-up e-mail that I received (with names changed to protect the guilty, as in all the examples in this book) after I started the registration process for an upcoming event but didn't complete the process. It is intended to make a sale (get me to register), but instead it convinces me that the company doesn't care whether I register or not, oh, and that it hires morons.

```
Dear sue Hershkowitz-coore,

We noticed that you visited the Planning for the
Cactus Convention Association but did not register.
If you would like to registering now, you may go to:
https://www.one-stop-cactus.com. If you have charged
your mind or did not intend to register, please do
not contract us, the information you entered will be
automatically deleted after 24 hours.

You can re-register at and point after this 24 hours
by going to CCA's web site and follow these links to
the registration page.

Thank you!

CCA Registrar
```

Clearly, "Registrar" (whoever that might be!) never bothered to complete the vital third step in the writing process (or even sixth grade) and has no worry that I will either "contract" them or "charge" my mind. "Registrar's" professionalism is nonexistent, and because Registrar is writing on behalf of the association, by extension, its professionalism is highly suspect, too. This writer lost the sale at "Dear sue."

Later in this book, we'll talk about reframing messages to help you present negative messages in neutral, acceptable terms. We'll cover strategies for writing in a customer-centric, user-friendly manner. We'll eliminate outdated, useless language and replace it with word tracks that are conversational, persuasive, and easy to understand and act upon. We'll discuss how social media has affected the way people read and how brevity and authenticity are vital for success. Eventually, you'll consider all these techniques during this final stage (and they will become like second nature to you). Right now, we'll look at some easy, fundamental changes that will improve the quality of your e-mail.

The revision and proofing step is nirvana for the analytical portion of your brain. This is when it gets to say to you, "Really? You're really going to write that?" I love this step because it gives you the opportunity to change whatever doesn't track, eliminate words and sentences that distract from the point, clarify sentences that say something other than what you mean (or could be interpreted to mean something that you don't), and correct typos and other embarrassing errors. This check step is when you get to swap words and clean up your e-mail. More than anything, though, the third step offers you the chance to show recipients that you respect their time and that you care enough about them to actually take the time to pay attention to details that will make it easy for them to read and respond.

How "perfect" does your e-mail need to be to engage your reader and extend your brand image? The answer depends on your brand reputation, or what you would like it to be. If you represent a company that is traditional, touts its attention to detail, provides luxurious service, and lives or dies by its level of customer service (and especially if your product or service appeals to an over-40-year-old demographic), your e-mail had better be Perfect. On the other hand, if your brand is more hip and edgy and you demonstrate that in your other collateral and your Web site, your accepted work style is laid back, and you appeal to a mostly under-40-year-old buyer (or those who wish they were), your e-mail only needs to be perfect.

E-mail, by its nature, is intended to be more casual than the quickly dying-out standard mail message. (Don't bury your pens yet, though; part of selling is getting noticed, and sending an occasional message that is delivered by a means other than electronically can still have stand-out value.) Also, most people are willing to allow writers an occasional slup of the thimb, um, slip of the thumb. (What was that about those without sin casting the first stone?)

Sending a sales message with typos, however, can relay an unintended message to your prospect: that you don't care enough to pay attention to the details, that you're too busy to do so, or that your message is so boring that even *you* don't want to take the time to read through it for accuracy. Depending on what you're selling (does attention to detail factor into your service or product?), prospects may judge your ability to deliver not on what you say but on your ability to demonstrate your flawless attention to detail. (An independent meeting planner lost a bid because she sent a proposal that she had based on another client with similar needs, with the Microsoft Word corrections showing. The worst part was that the planner couldn't see the correction marks on her own screen—but the customer could! The prospect rejected the bid, explaining that it was the planner's job to pay attention to those details!)

Also, correct spelling and proper punctuation help your reader read in the same way that a stoplight helps a driver drive. Proper punctuation quickly and effortlessly (for them) lets them know your intent. *Fine. Fine! Fine?* Each says different things, and without the proper mark, your customer is likely to pick up a wrong meaning. Attention to standards of grammar and punctuation makes it easy for your reader to stay in tune with your thinking.

MISS STEAKS EYE KIN KNOT SEA

Misspelled words can stop a reader in her tracks.

Have you ever noticed how easy it is to spot an error in an e-mail that you receive, yet not see the same error in your own message? That's because you're seeing the other e-mail with a fresh eye and actually reading it. Because we know what our message says, if we just skim and scroll as we check for correctness, we're likely to miss our errors. We even miss seeing the red or green lines that our software kindly adds for our consideration.

You may be familiar with this explanation:

THE PWEOR OF THE HMUAN MNID
Aoccdrnig to rscheearch at Cmabrigde Uinervtisy, it deosn't mttaer in waht oredr the ltteers in a word are, the olny iprmoatnt tihng is taht the frist and lsat ltteer be in the rghit pclae. The rset can be a taotl mses and you can sitll raed it wouthit porbelm. Tihs is bcuseae the huamn mnid deos not raed ervey lteter by istlef, but the wrod as a wlohe. Amzanig huh?   —Anonymous

✦✦✦

The more adept you are at reading, the more likely you are to send e-mails with typos and other errors. Good readers have learned to skim and still comprehend. This is awesome when you are reading mail that was sent to you, but it prevents you from proofing efficiently. You see words and phrases as a whole, rather than each letter.

For a laugh, here are a few examples of actual e-mail mistakes. (E-mail me your favorite examples so I can include them in my next book):

- Mary, the First Shift nurse, in setting up her signature line, accidentally (I'm just guessing this was inadvertent) omitted the letter *f* from the word *Shift*.
- An island country's Ministry of Tourism e-mailed a sales letter to 5,000 meeting professionals that the country was pursuing for potential business. The message was supposed to invite the meeting professionals "to the shores" of the country. The e-mail writer, however, left off the first letter *s* and instead invited them to "experience the hores of the island." (It was said that tourism skyrocketed, just not the kind the ministry wanted. The woman who wrote the e-mail for the minister was fired.)
- An e-mail from a nonprofit requested donations to lower the "morality" rate. (Not only will I donate to that, I'll even drink to that!) The "mortality" rate is what the organization wanted to lower.
- A southwestern state sent an e-mail to thousands of people inviting them to attend a "Pubic Executive Program." Of course it spell-checked perfectly. (I heard attendance was the best ever!)
- Bob, a general manager, received an e-mail from a vendor that started with "Hi Boob." Quite endearing.
- And my personal favorite: a sales manager at a hotel wrote to a prospect: "Thank you for the opportunity to *hose* your group." Italics mine.

Believe me, these are funny only if you aren't the person who wrote them. I once sent an e-mail that said "I lie" instead of "I like." My assistant misspelled "courtesy discount" on an agreement, preferring "curtsy." (That's a very deep discount, preferred only by debutantes.) A client e-mailed that she would make "aggravation at the hotel for me." I think she meant "a reservation."

Oh, and don't even get me started on not paying attention to the spelling of the name in the "To" line. After staying up really late to complete a proposal for a potential new client, I rewarded my perseverance by writing an e-mail to a friend asking her if she agreed that it was time for me to break up with the man I was dating. I was, shall we say, extremely graphic about the reasons I thought it was time to break up. Then instead of sending the e-mail to my friend, I sent the e-mail to the last address sent to, the potential new client. In the morning, I received a brief two-sentence e-mail from him that read: "I concur. Break up." And no, I did not book the business! Lesson learned: write the recipient's name last, after proofing the rest of the document, and pay attention to what actually populates the "To" field.

In November 2009, the Society of Human Resource Managers asked 498 human resource professionals for their reactions to typos in e-mail. A whopping 58 percent said that a typo was a "deal breaker," and 41 percent said that it was "somewhat of a problem." When I mentioned this research at a workshop, one attendee pointed out that human resource folks usually read e-mails from people who are job seeking, so "of course they'd expect them to take the extra time to make it perfect." Here's a tip: when you are in sales, you are always looking for a job.

Limit the possibility of major embarrassment or disappointment by applying these ideas during your check step:

- Change the look of your document when you proof it so that your eye can see the letters and not just the words. Modify the screen background color, font color, or font type style. If you always type with a white screen background, change it to yellow. The more out of the ordinary you make your document look to your own eyes, the more likely you'll be to *read* it and spot your errors.

- Change the pattern you use to read your words. Read from the last word of your message to the first. This practice also helps you see your document with fresh eyes by forcing you to look at and see each individual word.
- Partner with a trusted colleague. Swear each other to secrecy and use each other's eyes to catch the errors.
- Wait an hour or more and reread your message. You'll be amazed at how clearly you can see after a break. (This tip is particularly good if you're writing a message that requires sensitivity. More on this in later chapters.)

◆ ◆ ◆

Throw a critical eye on your writing after you've completed your message and before you hit Send. You'll thank me.

MOBILE DOESN'T MEAN MESSY

A question I'm commonly asked is: what about mobile? Answer: yes. If you're writing a business e-mail, the check step applies to messages written on a mobile device, too.

There are exceptions, of course. If you're dealing with a crisis (your customer is in the midst of a meeting and needs an answer urgently), the only thing that matters is the information.

If the flight attendant is about to confiscate your phone because the plane is taxiing and you're still typing because you promised to send your client the information before you left, just do the best you can. You can explain later if you were blunt or unpolished. But unless you are dealing with a crisis, business writing rules apply just as much to e-mails sent from a smartphone as they do to e-mails sent from your computer. In fact, even if you're texting a customer or posting on her Facebook page, do it right! Whenever you are communicating for business purposes, represent yourself as the professional you are and pay attention to the details.

Some people have been tricked into thinking that the default message set up on their mobile device is meant to grant permission for typos or less than clear sentences. Um, no. That message that comes programmed into your phone that adds, "Sent from my (fill in the blank here)" to your e-mails was never intended to be a disclaimer or to grant absolution. It started as a clever marketing tool so that every time you sent a message, you'd advertise the brand. Too many of us bought into it, being only too happy to let others know how cool we are for having a (fill in the blank). If you still have that marketing message enabled, disable it now so that you're not ever tempted to use it as permission to take shortcuts with your sales strategy, manners, or attention to detail.

◆ ◆ ◆

If you're trying to sell, especially when your client doesn't know you well, make it easy for him—and those that he might forward your message to—to think well of you. Type right!

ELIMINATE THE BORING STUFF

The critical check step, as mentioned, is more than reading for correctness. It's also checking for clarity and conciseness.

In the last few chapters, we planned and created. Now, we'll apply the failure-proof step.

The e-mail to BC, your trade show prospect, was written like this:

```
Hi BC,

Hope your trip was great, and I have to admit to
being a bit jealous! London! How cool is that! I've
always wanted to shop in those boutiques on Carnaby
Street (though I doubt I can afford them).
```

```
I appreciate your thinking of me to do X for you.
Here are the alternatives that might work for you:

A . . .

B . . .

C, your requested option, can't be accomplished
until September 9, and I know that is about 9 days
too late for you. We also might be able to expedite
shipment for you at an additional cost of $$$. I'll
need to check further on this if this is an option
you wish to pursue.

What will work best? Please let me know which option
is best for you, or if you have another idea, and
I'll follow through as soon as I receive your e-mail.
Please let me know.
```

Here is what the message was to accomplish:

1. *Why?* To provide a solution to her request.
2. *What?* Here are three possible solutions: A, B, and C.
3. *Accomplish?* Build a trusting relationship.
4. *Next step?* She e-mails me to tell me which option is best for her.
5. *Delighter?* She can count on me to follow through as soon as I receive her decision.

You've planned it and written it, and now you're about to perfect it. To create an e-mail that is concise and clear, review the message to determine whether all the points that need to be covered to achieve your goal are covered in the most concise fashion. Is information included that the recipient is likely not to be interested in and will skip anyway? Is there anything that might distract the reader from the selling (or buying) message? Beyond editing for basic mistakes, what can you do to clarify your message and show respect for your reader's needs and time? You might send a final version that looks like this:

```
Hi BC,

Good news! There are several alternatives that might
work so that you can do X:

A . . .

B . . .

C, your requested option, can be expedited to you
at a cost of $$$, or we can have it for you by
September 9 with no additional charges.

What will work best? As soon as you e-mail your
preferred option, I'll follow through and you can
relax knowing it's taken care of. Also, please
provide credit card information if you'd like us to
expedite the shipment.

Safe and productive travels, and I look forward to
receiving your preference so I can take care of this
for you.
```

How would you refine the Pupsville message? Here is what the writer wanted to accomplish:

1. *Why?* To create excitement about the prospect's highly successful golf events and meetings in Pupsville.
2. *What?* You can expect great attendance when you schedule a meeting in Pupsville. Attendees love coming here!
3. *Accomplish?* To pique the prospect's interest so that he will either (decide which of these you want before writing)
   a. Accept a call
   b. Respond to the e-mail
   c. Click on a link for more info
4. *Next step?* I call him Thursday.
5. *Delighter?* He can drive attendance to his next association meeting and get a sleeve of cool golf balls, too.

It may be helpful to reread what was written in Chapter 3 to determine for yourself how the message can be made stronger, more persuasive, and easier to read. Here is a revision for you to consider:

```
Hi Name,

If your goal is to select a meeting destination that
drives attendance and delights your members, you may
have found the perfect spot!

When attendees and guests learn that the meeting is
in Pupsville, they'll be excited to attend. With the
amazing variety of recreational options, including
fabulous, world-renowned golf, you can expect your
attendance to practically double! Additionally, you
can rely on Pupsville to provide your members with
a unique learning environment that supports and
enhances your meeting agenda.

I'll phone you Thursday morning to discuss fresh
ideas to create a meeting that is fun, memorable,
and meaningful.
```

◆ ◆ ◆

The three-step process (planning, doing, and checking) saves up to 80 percent of the time you spend writing. It also makes you look brilliant, professional, and polished. Count on selling more, too.

PART TWO

◆◆◆

THE PSYCHOLOGY OF PERSUASIVE WRITING

In the end, the customer doesn't know, or care, if you are small or large as an organisation. She or he only focuses on the garment hanging on the rail in the store.

—GIORGIO ARMANI

Successful sales writing takes more than knowing how to apply the mechanics of writing (although it is hard to write to sell if you don't know e-mail etiquette and business writing fundamentals). Successful sales writing requires an understanding of the psychology of the written word, how readers read, and how they react to various words and messages. It requires knowing which words and what approach to use to persuade the reader to open your message and read it, when her other choices—to delay reading or delete the message—

may be easier for her. Successful sales writing requires an understanding of how to frame an idea so that it piques the reader's interest and motivates her to act.

High-performing sales professionals guide their readers on a journey, and their readers gladly follow. This section focuses on how you can position your message so that it invites prospects, customers, and clients, and also colleagues, counterparts, managers, and staff members, to not just read your e-mail but be persuaded by your message to take the next step. Discover how you can communicate in writing to make it easy for your readers to say yes to you.

CHAPTER 5

◆◆◆

CREATE A SELLING MESSAGE THAT BUILDS SALES

Wherever smart people work, doors are unlocked.

—STEVE WOZNIAK

Have you heard the one about three people and the corned beef sandwiches?

A woman runs into the deli and orders her sandwich quickly. She never takes her eyes off her BlackBerry, scrolling furiously; she also keeps looking at her watch impatiently while the counterperson piles the sandwich high with corned beef. She needs to get back to work, and she wants her sandwich a few seconds ago.

The next guy isn't in such a rush. He has an hour for lunch, and he plans to enjoy a leisurely meal. In fact, today he is doing something that is totally out of character. Instead of his usual roast beef, he orders a corned beef sandwich. It's been a while since he has had something other than roast beef, and he has an hour to savor it.

The third person isn't rushing at all. He usually doesn't eat lunch, or much else, for that matter. Today, while he was panhandling, someone gave him a ten-dollar bill. "Have a good meal," she said as she handed him the money. Clutching the bill, he walked up and down the street, wondering which restaurant would treat him okay and feed him well. Finally deciding on the deli, he orders and pays for his meal and sits down to relish a gourmet corned beef sandwich.

According to Ron Karr, in his "Titan Principle Sales E-Report," when 13-year-old Joshua Feldman told that story at his bar mitzvah, his point was to show how everyone looks at the bar mitzvah experience differently. In life, we each have our own agenda for everything we do.

As sales professionals, managers, and leaders, the better we understand those individual agendas—and write to them—the more successful we are. The challenge that most salespeople have, though, is that they love their product, service, or idea too much. Our product or idea or service is special and significant to us, and we're excited to tell the other person about its extraordinary capabilities and whiz-bang features. It's only by focusing on the importance of those features, the benefits to our readers, however, that we can possibly get *them* excited. Instead of writing from our own perspective (rushed, calm, or hungry) or about our own need (quick necessity, peaceful meal, or satisfying nutrition), successful sales pros turn it around and write about what's in it for the buyer.

All over the world, when I ask, "What or why is your customer buying?" workshop attendees typically answer with a feature puke. "Space, dates, and rates," the hotel salespeople respond. Those selling financial services tell me (oh so cleverly!) that their customers are buying "financial expertise," and pharmaceutical reps say "drugs" (which at least makes me smile).

◆ ◆ ◆

The only reason people choose to buy from you is their own reason.

Customers typically don't need the actual widget that you sell; they need the result that they hope the widget will bring. Regardless of what you sell, it's the benefit of what you sell that they buy. (Even if you sell winter coats, this is true. No one necessarily *needs* a winter coat. What people *need* is a way to keep warm. What many *want* is a way to not only keep out the cold but look fashionable [cute, sexy, rich, young, polished, professional, hip, cool, and so on] as well, and the winter coats you sell help them do that. If they just wanted a winter coat, any coat would do, even their old, ripped, outdated one.)

Here is another example. I sell sales training, but that isn't what my clients buy. They don't spend money for training. They spend money to make money through more skillful selling. They buy improved results: increased revenue, higher profits, converted leads, and more prospects in the funnel. (The more I can help them see the results they'll receive, the easier it is for them to buy.) They buy more focused, invested, competent employees. They buy their success—not my programs.

Before you can write great sales e-mail messages, it's important that you evaluate the outcome or solution that you sell.

◆◆◆

Sell what matters to the buyer.

John Caples, a (dead) advertising genius who created, arguably, the most successful advertisement of the twentieth century, said, "The most frequent reason for unsuccessful advertising is that advertisers are so full of their own accomplishments (the world's best seed!) that they forget to tell us why we should buy (the world's best lawn!)." This is also the most frequent reason for unsuccessful sales writing.

Your core message—your selling message—is the solution to the challenge that your prospect is having. It's the benefits of the features that you offer. Your core selling message is not the square footage of your ballroom, how many dealerships or distributors you have, how many years you've been in business, or the prestigious name of your company. Your core selling message is what those features will do for your prospects.

SO WHAT IS YOUR CORE MESSAGE?

A challenge that is critical to sales writing success is to step away from your product or service and examine the core of your sales message. Ask yourself (and be gut honest): *What exactly is the value proposition that I offer prospects?* Be careful not to list what you offer. Instead, consider the value buyers receive from what you offer. From a sales writing perspective, here's what happens when you don't have a definitive answer to that question: your message rambles, is irrelevant to the reader, and usually gets quickly deleted.

To determine your core message, answer these important questions:

- What pains, challenges, needs, or wants does my customer/ prospect/client have that my product, service, or idea soothes, answers, improves, or heals?
- What pains, challenges, needs, or wants does my customer's customer have that my product, service, or idea soothes, answers, improves, or heals?
- What solutions do I offer to my customers?

Imagine that you sell premium dog food to veterinarians. To determine your core message or value proposition, you'll want to consider the following:

1. *What are the pains, challenges, needs, or wants that veterinarians have that my high-end dog food answers?* Without spending too much time on this example (unless you sell high-end dog food to vets, in which case you should), it's easy to imagine what vets' challenges are: they need to make more money and build their business, and they don't want to jeopardize their ethical or professional standing to do it.

2. *What are the pains, challenges, needs, or wants that veterinarians' customers (the people, not the animals) have that your premium dog food answers?* Veterinarians' customers are challenged by a lack of knowledge ("What is the best thing to give to my sweet angel?"), a lack of confidence ("Am I doing the best thing for

'baby'?"), and often a lack of time ("Work, family, and now the dog . . . just make it easy for me").

3. *What are the solutions that you offer?* You offer just about everything a vet needs for everlasting happiness! You have the solution to increased income, professional health care, and happy, satisfied, loyal patients who refer others. Through your food product and accompanying research, you help the vet offer knowledge that will make the patient (the person) feel confident that he is doing the best for his fur kid. You offer a timesaving solution that saves the patient inconvenience, stress, and a hassle. These patients will love the doctor because Fluffy, Fido, and Fifi will have a shiny coat and stay healthy. Fido's mom feels great about her smart purchase, she saves time and stress by not having to make another stop to pick up the food, and because she is so delighted (and feels so safe and smart with her choice), she recommends her vet to all her pet-loving friends.

The sales message I'd send to the veterinarian, if I were selling high-end dog food, wouldn't be about the food (although I'd certainly provide a hyperlink in my e-mail to my company Web site so that the vet can easily access the information that he needs to make a well-informed decision, and I'd provide a PDF attachment, too). The e-mail would discuss how he, the vet, can increase his income, provide the best care, easily earn referrals, and keep his patients loyal. The value proposition isn't the food (although, of course, without the product—the feature—there would be no value). The food's value proposition is in enabling the vet to become the most loved, trusted, and successful vet in town!

Once you determine exactly what your core message is, consider it your "go-to" statement. For instance, when someone asks you what you do, the best response isn't, "I sell premium dog food," "I'm a sales manager for the ABC Company," or "I'm a sales trainer." The best response is an answer that answers their unasked question, "What do you do that matters to me and that I can understand?" By answering their question with more than just your title, and with a focus on them, you're likely to initiate a meaningful conversation. An answer like: "You know how veterinarians are always looking for the best health-care options for their patients and for additional smart income streams? What I do is offer a product that patients and their people love and drives additional revenue for you."

◆◆◆

Think in terms of your value proposition (the outcome of buying your product). This makes it easier for you to write your sales message in a persuasive, comfortable, conversational manner.

Here is another example to clarify this concept.

If you're a sales trainer and your direct prospect is a corporate meeting planner, what are her greatest challenges or pains? She wants to look smart and appear competent to her attendees and other stakeholders. She wants to feel confident that her choice of sales trainers will please attendees and provide ROI for her organization. She wants her attendees to learn new skills to sell more.

What are the "pains" the corporate planner's customers have? Before answering this question, it's important to think of who the customers are. In addition to the participants in the training, her customers might include the CEO, the CFO, the director of sales, the human resource manager, a board of directors and shareholders, and so on. When you consider the wants, needs, and challenges of each of these stakeholders, you may discover that you need more than one value proposition (because different stakeholders value different things).

Here is an example of a core message that the sales trainer might use to alleviate one of her buyer's "pains"—wondering and worrying if attendees will experience value in an enjoyable manner and be happy with her choice: *You can feel confident that your attendees will laugh while they learn practical, easy-to-apply selling skills. They'll leave prepared to convert prospective leads into solid, profitable business.*

◆ ◆ ◆

If your core message seems salesy, sounds cheesy, or feels over-the-top, start again. In sales writing, conveying authenticity is vital. Don't shout your message; use your "inside voice."

When creating your core message, start with the word *you* or *your*. You'll have an easier time writing a statement that is about your prospect and meaningful to him if you do. It may not be easy to divorce yourself from your passion for your product, but it will be worth the struggle to direct that passion toward your prospect and his success. The more you focus on what the prospect experiences or enjoys as a result of what you sell, the easier it will be for you to write winning sales e-mails.

A highly esteemed marketing guru, Ted Levitt, was right when he said, "People don't buy a quarter-inch drill bit, they buy a quarter-inch hole. You've got to study the hole, not the drill. The drill is just the solution for it."

EMOTION CREATES THE SALE; LOGIC JUSTIFIES IT

Neuromarketing research shows that our brains are wired to buy with emotion and justify the purchase with logic. Whenever I fall in love with a cute pair of shoes (or a lampshade, coffee drink, paint color, or whatever) and then notice the price (oh, my!), without any conscious effort on my part, I start justifying the expense. I consider all the places I can wear those shoes (or how long I'll keep the lampshade and how long I've had the last outdated, ugly one). By the time my brain is finished justifying all the places those shoes will take me, they are the bargain of the century!

Most of us buy with our heart and justify with our head. Yet most salespeople sell the other way around.

You may remember a 2009 *Mad Men* television episode in which Don Draper, an advertising executive, created a marketing campaign for a slide projector (the show is set in the early 1960s) that was then being called the Kodak "Wheel." In Draper's awesome sales presentation to highly skeptical clients, he doesn't mention how many slides the projector can accommodate, or any other *logical* reason to buy the Wheel. Instead, he engages his prospects with emotion and story. By renaming the Wheel a "carousel," he likens what it does to "a time machine that goes backwards and forwards." While clicking through slides of a loving family, he says that the projector "travels the way a child does, round and round" like a "carousel." He "creates a sentimental bond" between a loving family's photos and the Kodak Carousel. (If you haven't seen this priceless episode, you can Google it.)

◆ ◆ ◆

What is your sentimental bond? What is the feeling that your product provokes in your prospect?

It's true that at some point (sooner rather than later), some customers may want to understand the features that you offer. (This isn't always important. If I want the shoes, I don't want to know that they were painstakingly hand-dyed or that they are made from Brazilian cow leather. True, these features might make it easier for some people to justify the purchase, but it would be TMI [too much information] for me. I don't want to think of people sitting in some sweatshop somewhere hand-dying my shoes and making five cents a day, or of the poor cow who gave its life for dumb shoes! The shoes are cute, and I had loved them, but thank you, with all that information, no, I have other shoes at home and won't be buying these. Now, had the description of the shoes mentioned that Carrie Underwood has them in three colors, Halle Berry bought two in every color, and they were featured in *Vogue* last month, that would be the emotional clincher.)

Don't rush to write about features. Instead, provide links so that your buyer can educate himself further, if he wishes. When writing a sales e-mail, focus more on engaging your buyer with an evocative, authentic, and relevant core message. By doing so, you'll boost your ability to persuade and influence the sale.

INFLUENCE WITH BENEFICIAL OUTCOMES

Here is a short list of customer benefits. As you read the list, think about how you can create brief but potent emotional pictures to help your buyers sense how happy they'll be—what they can aspire to—when they use, own, or choose your product.

- **Save time.** What will they be able to do with the time they save? Will they have more time with their children, more time to take good care of themselves, more time for romance? Create the picture. Tell the story.
- **Save money.** What can they do with the money they save? Help them imagine the benefits they'll derive from saving money.
- **Enjoy value.** How? What picture can you paint of them experiencing your value proposition?
- **Feel good.** Help them imagine this.
- **Sound smart.** What will others be likely to say about their competence? Paint the picture for them.
- **Look good.** They, too, can be a size 2 and look like Cameron Diaz!
- **Increase profits.** Be as specific as possible, and help them envision what that will look like and feel like.
- **Drive revenue.** How much? How will it feel?
- **Bolster sales.** How much? How will that happen?
- **Have fun.** Help them see themselves having fun.
- **Experience less stress.** Help them envision their stress-free life.
- **Feel relaxed, energized, and happy.** Help them visualize it.
- **Feel secure and confident.** Explain what this could feel like to them.
- **Be safe.** What simple but meaningful analogy can you make?

- **Feel confident.** Describe what others will see in them. Describe what they can expect to see in themselves.
- **Maintain hope for a better (fill in the blank).** Help them see themselves reaching and achieving their dream.

As mentioned earlier, if your prospect can't achieve what you are putting in writing, stop writing. Using these ideas to trick your customer is, in my opinion, fraud. Offer aspirational benefits only if your product or service is able to provide the possibility. (It's okay if "actual weight loss will vary," as long as it's true that weight loss will occur if the directions are followed.) Paint accurate, genuine pictures of what is possible with your service, idea, or product.

When you can comfortably express your *authentic* core message, you are well on your way to writing successful e-mails that win business and convert leads. Determine whether it's corned beef or roast beef that's important to your buyer. Understand the motivation for ordering the corned beef, and you'll be more persuasive than you can possibly imagine!

◆ ◆ ◆

Spend your words on creating desire. Paint brief, aspirational word pictures. Make it easy for your customer to sense her authentic success.

CHAPTER 6

♦ ♦ ♦

CONNECT THE DOTS
TO SELL MORE

*With every experience, you alone are painting your own
canvas, thought by thought, choice by choice.*

—OPRAH WINFREY

Once you're prepared to present your sales message in terms of benefits and emotional, authentic outcomes, differentiating your product in the minds of your buyers in your e-mail messages becomes simple.

It's safe to say that most (although not all) buyers want to save money, feel confident, and experience less stress. Often, however, salespeople provide useless information (like the Brazilian cow leather in the previous chapter) or sell the wrong outcome to the buyer. Knowing what your specific buyer values makes it easy for you to connect the dots between what you offer and the solution he can receive from you.

♦ ♦ ♦

Your core message connects the dots between what you sell and what your customers buy.

Imagine that you are a hotel salesperson, and you've just received a lead—an RFP (request for proposal)—generated from your Web site. The RFP is only partially complete; the buyer has filled in the name of the association desiring the meeting space, the meeting dates required, the number of sleeping rooms needed, and the number of educational sessions planned. However, the section on your form that asks, "What matters to you when selecting a hotel for your group?" has been left blank, and so has budget.

Because you're an experienced sales professional, the first thing you do is Google the name of the association. You learn that it has 2,500 members and it has held its annual member meetings in hotels that are competitively priced with yours. Do you know what matters to the buyer?

Because this is an e-lead, you can't count on having a conversation with the buyer. (Also, you notice the words "Do not call" in bold type on every page of the RFP!) You'll need to rely on what you know, in general, about this type of buyer. What matters most to people who are planning associations' annual meetings? What are their needs, wants, and pains? What are their customers' needs? Finally, what are the solutions you offer to those needs and wants?

You can feel confident that they want the meeting to be successful for their attendees. You also are certain that their members attend the annual meeting to gain new perspectives and new skills and to network with counterparts in their industry. You also realize that if their members don't update their skills, they are not likely to survive in the industry (the pain).

This is a great start. Instead of just e-mailing to confirm that you have appropriate meeting space (feature), you might also explain how the configuration of your meeting space lends itself to convenient networking opportunities (benefit), making it easy for attendees to feel comfortable learning from one another and creating an even more valuable and productive meeting experience. You might explain how your environment is designed to support and enhance learning so that meeting attendees stay focused to derive the most from their meeting time. These responses connect the dots for your buyer.

By positioning your features so that the buyer's unasked questions are answered—Why will my meeting be successful here? How will you take away my pain?—you differentiate your offering and your e-mail. (Your competitors are busy writing about features like their 13,845 feet of available space or their distance from the airport!)

You may not want to stop there, however. By digging a bit deeper about what matters to the planner (buyer) of an association annual event, you can be even more persuasive and successful.

You can provide a value proposition that will be even more meaningful to such a planner by continuing to think from your buyer's perspective. You might come up with something like this: the meeting is a failure (definite pain) if attendance is small. In fact, the entire association (and the planner's job) could be in jeopardy if the meeting doesn't generate enough income to keep the association functioning and servicing its members.

With this in mind, consider your writing strategy:

1. *Why?* To excite the association planner about a hugely successful meeting (highly attended) at ABC Hotel.
2. *What?* You can count on great attendance because attendees love coming here.
3. *Accomplish?* Persuade the planner to agree to take my call.
4. *Next step?* Planner e-mails approval for my call or phones me.
5. *Delighter?* You, Ms. Planner, will hear additional ideas to ensure that your 2018 meeting beats all attendance records.

The e-mail you write to transmit your proposal might say

```
Hello Association Planner,

You can count on your 2018 XYZ Association annual
meeting being a huge success at the ABC Hotel! Your
preferred dates are available, and I've attached a
proposal for your consideration.
```

You can plan on increased attendance at your meeting when your members learn that you've selected the ABC. Attendees love coming here because they know they'll all be treated like VIPs, receive great value, and be in the center of all the action. Whether they want to discuss the day's activities in a serene atmosphere or prefer to recharge with exciting entertainment choices, it's all available within steps of our front door.

Name, to ensure that I've provided everything you need for an unforgettable event, may I phone you Tuesday? If you prefer, I'd be honored if you'd phone me (555-555-5555). My goal is to ensure that your 2018 meeting beats all attendance records!

I'll follow up with you as you suggest.

When you blend your core message with what matters to your prospect and make it plain to him that it's less about selling and more about offering him a solution to the challenges that he has, you will convert more leads and build more business. You won't need to worry about what your competition is offering because you'll set yourself apart and earn the right to advance to the next stage of buying (not selling!).

Make it easy for your prospects, customers, and clients to visualize their success in order to make it simple for them to choose your product or service. When you're the best at delivering the right information in the right way (their way), not only do you ensure your buyer's success, but you ensure your own.

◆ ◆ ◆

The more you connect the dots for your buyer, the less work she has to do, the easier you make it for her to choose you to supply her with what she needs.

Here is another example: You sell financial products, including insurance. Earlier today, you had a brief conversation with a woman after your Zumba class, and when you told her that you were in the middle of helping a client who had recently lost her husband, and that's why you were late to class, she asked you what you did. One word led to another, and she explained that she owns a small business and had recently been thinking about switching insurance agents and asked if you'd e-mail her some information. Before you could ask her any additional questions, her mobile rang. As she was fishing through her gym bag for the phone, she mentioned that she never hears from her current agent, that he doesn't even sign the preprinted birthday cards that he sends to her, and that she really should check to be sure she has the right coverage. She says she has been so busy with work and family that it's been years since she reviewed it. With that, she answers her call, writes her e-mail address on a slip of paper, hands it to you while talking, and waves good-bye.

I'm betting that you know exactly what matters to this buyer, and it has little to do with the insurance product you sell. Her pain is insecurity (lack of knowledge) and lack of attention (a supplier who takes her business for granted). What she needs may or may not be a different policy; what she wants is to have confidence in her decisions and trust in her provider. If you send her information about coverage, she won't read it (and will feel even worse about herself!). If, instead, you e-mail to help her feel safe and smart, you're likely to earn the right to advance to a meeting with her.

What will you say to her in your e-mail? The first thing to do, of course, is to plan your written message by considering your sales strategy:

1. *Why?* To help her feel confident and smart and safe about her insurance decisions.
2. *What?* You can feel confident that you've made smart decisions once I have reviewed your policy.
3. *Accomplish?* To start a trusting business relationship and to ask her to let me know when it might be convenient for her to set up a quick meeting.

4. *Next step?* She e-mails me with date and time.
5. *Delighter* She can relax, knowing that she has made informed insurance decisions.

You might e-mail her something like this:

```
Hi friend (but use her name!),

Thanks so much for taking a few minutes to talk with
me after Zumba class today, and I'm honored that
you've asked me for information. To ensure that you're
on the best path for your current and future needs,
I'd be delighted to review your current policies
because they may be absolutely perfect for you.
Please tell me when you'd like to meet—we can go for
a quick coffee before or after Zumba class, if that's
convenient for you. I want you to feel confident that
you've made smart decisions regarding your future.
```

Without planning, this sales message might have turned into an information dump. Instead, by taking a few seconds to think through what you really want to accomplish, your true purpose (to start a trusting business relationship and motivate her to take the next step) becomes apparent. You aren't sending useless information or coming across as just another person who is simply interested in making a sale.

In this example, you and your prospect already have an informal relationship, so it makes sense to keep that same tone. Also, because the prospect explained to you that she was quite busy, it's smart to turn over control of the meeting time to her, rather than suggesting alternative dates. You don't want to appear pushy (even if that isn't your intent—intent can too easily be misunderstood). Additionally, suggesting coffee doesn't seem overwhelming; your harried prospect is likely to say yes if she doesn't need to commit to a major step.

BUILD TRUST WITH THE WORDS YOU CHOOSE

Did you notice, in the Zumba e-mail, the words "I want you to feel confident that you've made smart decisions regarding your future"? Writing exactly what you want your reader to think (planting the seeds) works! People think about what they're told to think about.

◆ ◆ ◆

Make your writing powerful and persuasive. Tell your reader what he can expect from you. Plant positive thoughts, and your buyer will be likely to think positive thoughts. Plant doubt, and that is exactly what you'll get.

Here are additional phrases that engender trust:

- You can count on
- You can rely on
- You can feel confident about
- You can relax knowing
- You can depend on

Each of these phrases assures the buyer that he is in good hands. It explains the feelings and benefits that he can expect to receive from working with you. Just don't disappoint him.

CHAPTER 7

◆◆◆

BE LIKABLE TO WIN
THE BUSINESS

*Those of us who use love as a point of differentiation in
business will separate ourselves from our competitors just as
world-class distance runners separate themselves from the
rest of the pack trailing behind them.*

—TIM SANDERS, *LOVE IS THE KILLER APP*

Picture this: you are in the market for a widget. Because many companies sell widgets, all slightly different, yet strikingly similar, you spend a couple of hours researching your options. As you suspected, prices are pretty much the same across the board, and differences are minimal. You decide to send identical e-mails to two of the companies, one that has a long history of widget selling and another that is a younger upstart. You make a pact with yourself to give your business to the company that responds best.

Both companies respond in about the same amount of time and provide similar factual attachments. When you read the e-mails, however, you actually have the sense that one salesperson cares. The e-mail is only four brief sentences, but the message is personalized and the tone feels empathetic:

```
Hi You (but your name is used),

Thanks for asking for additional information! Making
the right choice when all widgets appear the same
can be confusing. I've attached the guidelines
and pricing to help you, and I am here to answer
additional questions. My mobile is 555-555-5555.
```

The other response was a bit shorter; it simply said: "Here is the information you requested."

Which company would *you* buy from?

The reality is that most products today look like fraternal (if not identical) twins. Often your only chance to stand out in a sea of sameness is in the e-mail you send to the prospect. You can differentiate yourself by communicating in a likable, authentic manner.

In a later chapter, we'll talk about how to write "negative messages" and still keep customers happy. For now, we'll focus on routine selling situations where it should be a snap to come across as likable, trustworthy, and empathetic.

WIN BUSINESS WITH THE WORDS YOU CHOOSE

It's been said that excellent customer service is hard to explain, but you know it when you see it. Likable sales writing is much the same. Yet, as with extraordinary service, there are certain characteristics that must be present for likability to exist.

Tim Sanders, in his book *The Likeability Factor: How to Boost Your L-Factor and Achieve Your Life's Dreams*, said that for someone to be seen as likable, four attributes need to be present: being friendly, relevant, empathetic, and real. Expressing these four characteristics is difficult enough to accomplish in conversation, where there are verbal and nonverbal cues and clues; in e-mail, it's even more challenging.

◆◆◆

Communicating likability in e-mail takes effort. It's not something that happens without practice and desire.

It doesn't take a scientist to know how easy it is to misread the writer's intentions in an e-mail. Yet it *is* now a proven fact. According to research conducted by Kristin Byron, assistant professor of management at the Whitman School of Management at Syracuse University, "Miscommunication in emails can be caused by senders' inability to accurately convey their intended meaning and by receivers' inability to perceive the senders' intended meaning." Exactly!

Further, in an article called "Egocentrism over E-Mail: Can We Communicate as Well as We Think?" published in the *Journal of Personality and Social Psychology,* Justin Kruger (New York University, Stern School of Business), Nicholas Epley (University of Chicago, Graduate School of Business), Jason Parker, and Zhi-Wen Ng (University of Illinois at Urbana–Champaign) found that it's our ego that keeps us from understanding how the other person will interpret our e-mail. It's extremely difficult, the researchers contend, to "detach oneself from one's own perspective when evaluating the perspective of someone else."

We read from our rushed, self-focused perspective. We can't hear the sender's inflection, we may not know her, and we don't bother to give her the benefit of the doubt. Writers should keep in mind how easy it is for their customers to decipher an incorrect message. What the writer intended as a positive e-mail is often perceived as simply neutral. And, according to the research just cited, in readers' heads, what the writer intends to be a neutral tone is often perceived as negative. Writing a likable e-mail is tough to do and crucially important to sales success.

How do you convey likability—friendliness, genuineness, concern, and relevance—in an e-mail?

First, authentically care about the other person's success. If you don't, it won't matter what words you use. People can smell a rat a mile away (and tweet about it forever).

Next, choose words purposefully to help your recipient feel safe and smart. To create likability, make your word choices reflect on his success rather than on your sale.

APPLY THESE TIPS TO BOOST LIKABILITY

Here are some additional specific, practical tips to ensure that your prospect interprets your message the way you intended it:

- **Create a message that genuinely revolves around your prospect.** Do you recall the scene in the movie *Beaches* when Bette Midler is talking with a friend about herself, and when she realizes that she has monopolized the conversation, she says, "But enough about me, let's talk about you . . . what do you think about me?" That's not what you want to do in your sales message!
- **Use more *you* and *your* words than *I* or *me* words.** When you use *we*, be sure that it truly reflects a partnership between you and your prospect, and not just between you and your imaginary friend. Count up the number of times you use the words *I, my, our,* and your organization's name. Then compare that number with how many times you use the words *you* and *your.* This "sales math" pretty much spells out where your focus lies.
- **Reflect the prospect's style.** It doesn't show a high degree of empathy to respond with just one or two words to an e-mail that clearly took the writer time and thought to write. Responding with only "Got it" to an e-mail that was thoughtfully and painstakingly written is just rude. When responding, take your cue from the other person. On the other hand, if your recipient is the one to write two words to your five sentence e-mail, take their cue by tightening your message back to them.

- **Start with something that matters to your reader.** Show your prospect where your focus is by immediately writing about something that is relevant to his success, not to yours. Avoid these self-centered beginnings:
  - I wanted to follow up with you regarding . . .
  - I am pleased to inform you . . .
  - I am writing to introduce myself/I would like to introduce myself . . .
  - I hope this message finds you well/having a great day
  - I am trying to contact you . . .
  - It is my pleasure to write to you to . . .
  - I am very excited about writing to you . . .
  - It was a pleasure speaking with you . . .
- **Be positive.** Say what is possible instead of what isn't. Choose positive phrasing (this is possible when . . .) rather than negative (this isn't possible because . . .). Always provide your sales solution before telling someone what you can't do.
- **Be brief but not blunt.** Every word you use should help the buyer feel confident and comfortable buying from you and should contribute to the clarity and courtesy of the message.
- **Be authentic!** Eliminate fake "rapport-building" statements at both the beginning and the end of the e-mail. An all-too-common throwaway phrase like "How are you today?" doesn't establish rapport. It shows the customer that you couldn't think of a more significant, reader-focused way to begin. (If you really cared how she was, you'd call.)

  "Have a great day!" is equally bad as a closing line. Whenever a sales message begins or closes with these fake signs of caring, it's a sure sign that the writer was aware that the message wasn't friendly enough and was hopeful that this gratuitous show of caring would cover for a lack of substance.

  "Happy Friday" is another phrase to avoid. The implication (Yay! It's finally Friday and I'm out of here!) doesn't send the right message to a prospect that you're trying to woo and convince to buy your product.

◆◆◆

Even when you have an engaging relationship with your customer, consider how those whom she might copy and forward your e-mail to might interpret your intentions. Better safe than sorry!

- **Close with your delighter.** Instead of ending your message with a process-driven or procedural statement, close with a positive thought, something that is meaningful to the reader. Help him to like you.

Here are some examples:
Instead of

```
Once again, I look forward to working with you (a
statement about the writer).
```

Try

```
Your attendees will thank you for selecting ABC
Hotel (a statement that is meaningful to the
recipient and a positive thought).
```

Instead of

```
If you have additional questions, please call me at
555-555-5555 (procedural).
```

Try

```
I'll phone you Tuesday morning to discuss additional
options to save you time and money (meaningful to
the recipient and a positive thought).
```

Instead of

```
I look forward to your response (procedural and
self-focused).
```

Try

```
I'll follow up with you as you suggest. You can
count on outstanding quality and top-notch service
(meaningful to the recipient and a positive
thought).
```

- **Keep your message concise.** Prospects are just as busy as you are. Respect their time by taking *your* time to filter out the information that doesn't affect their success. Reread your message in the check step while asking yourself, "Does this matter to her?"
- **Eliminate outdated phrases.** Here is a brief list of words and phrases that are not only "so 2008," but in some cases are so 1953!
  As per your request
  Attached please find
  Basically
  In other words
  May I suggest
  More than happy
  Needless to say
  Please feel free
  Please do not hesitate to call
- **Avoid being sucked into using terms that are clichéd and overused.** Here is a list of words that should be eliminated from business writing:
  Reach out
  Touch base
  Thought leader
  Join the conversation
  Fast-paced

At the end of the day
With that said
Paradigm
New paradigm
Take the discussion offline
Push the envelope
Think outside the box
Out of pocket
At the end of the day

This abbreviated list comes from a Meeting Professionals International LinkedIn discussion group, but there are many other phrases that are so cool, they aren't.

• **Eliminate words that make your reader feel stupid.** This includes about 90 percent of words that end in *-ly*:
Basically (Do you need to dumb down the message for them?)
Honestly (What was everything else?)
Obviously (If it is, there is no need to say it. Insulting.)
Evidently (Ditto)
Clearly (Ditto)

◆◆◆

It's smart business to go out of your way to present your sales message, and yourself, likably. Sell the prospect on you first.

CHAPTER 8

◆◆◆

USE SOCIAL MEDIA TRENDS TO WRITE MORE PERSUASIVE E-MAILS

You can be professional while also "keeping it real" with your customers. By interacting with customers in a less formal way, you'll build a strong human connection that helps build brand loyalty.

—DAVID HAUSER, COFOUNDER OF GRASSHOPPER

"Keeping it real" has never been more important. It's not that writing in a pompous or inauthentic way has ever been a particularly clever sales strategy, but today, just the thought of a salesperson writing to impress, rather than express, is insulting and silly.

Keeping a sales e-mail "real" means creating a message that is easy to read, genuine, and relevant. Think about the clear, crisp, concise style of any business blog you enjoy reading. Write your e-mails in the same engaging manner.

HOW SOCIAL NETWORKING TRENDS AFFECT SALES

Regardless of how you may feel about social media, its impact on how the world communicates is undeniable. Successful bloggers, tweeters, and friends have learned how to communicate to engage readers and build followers. They keep it real by providing timely, relevant, authentic information in a succinct (140 characters, anyone?) and interesting way. Smart, successful sales professionals do the same.

Applying writing ideas learned from social media will help you write e-mails that are more engaging and more financially rewarding.

Would You Say It Like This to Your Reader?

Use conversational words. Prospects want to feel comfortable with you; it's the first step in building a trusting relationship. The ironic part is that they'll feel comfortable with you only when you make them feel comfortable about themselves. Choose words that your reader doesn't have to think about or stumble on. Using "the conversational test," an idea that the *Wall Street Journal* proposed years ago, still applies: "If you wouldn't say it, don't write it." That long-ago article said that too many people believe that "puffy sentences will make them appear more educated or more polished" than they feel they really are. That's still true today.

Trust yourself to use the conversational test. Ask yourself: would I say it like this to my reader if I were talking to her instead of e-mailing her? If you wouldn't, don't even consider writing it. (Just remember: not everything you can say, should you write. Write the way you speak, and then clean it up—check it!) Don't Google thesaurus.com for a replacement word. The comfortable word, the word you can trust to mean what you know it means and what your reader knows it means, is your best bet.

I am not suggesting that you purposely write for the most simple among us. Rather, in an information-overloaded world, the best way to get your message across is to present it simply. The longer the sentence and the fancier the words, the longer it will take your customer to understand the message. A sentence like, "I will help you book more business and sell more products," gets through the clutter. A more "erudite" statement like, "I will assist you in achieving greater profitability and transacting additional revenue through viable product sales" (I used the thesaurus for that) is ridiculous. Choose the clear, conversational word to avoid distracting your prospect from the real message.

◆◆◆

Prospects buy from people who sound like, um, people.

Fanny Brice's advice is as true for writing today as it was for a much simpler time: "Let the world know you as you are," she said, "not as you think you should be—because sooner or later, if you're posing, you will forget the pose and then where are you?"

Prefer the conversational word to the fancier version. Here is a list of pompous words and their more natural replacements:

Above-mentioned	Above
Accordingly	So
Cease	Stop
Cognizant	Aware
Commend	Praise, congratulate
Conclude	End, close
Construct	Make
Deem	Think, consider
Discontinue	Stop, end
Disincentive	Penalty
Effectuate	Effect
Endeavor	Try
Formulate	Form, think
Herewith	Enclosed, attached
Initiate	Begin, start
Preventative	Preventive

Prioritize	Rank, rate, list
Subsequent to	After, following
Substantiate	Support, back up
Sufficient	Enough
Ubiquitous	Widespread, all over
Utilize	Use

Use words that your reader will relate to and understand. Stephen King, in his book *On Writing: A Memoir of the Craft*, recommends using easy, conversational language regardless of the type of writing you're doing. "One of the really bad things you can do to your writing is to dress up the vocabulary, looking for long words because you're a little bit ashamed of your short ones. This is like dressing up a household pet in evening clothes." Keep your words short and to the point to impress your reader with your ideas.

Is This Your Voice?

Use your own voice. Your customers want to feel that they know the real you, and your writing should sound like it came from a breathing person, not your corporate PR department. Your customer wants to feel that she has a relationship with a human being—with you. This happens most easily when you don't sound like everyone else or anyone else, but just like yourself.

Of course, it's important that you keep your company's culture in mind when you write. Your writing voice sets the tone or mood of the e-mail and should reflect your organizational brand. Using the right tone is like being dressed appropriately. When business casual was first adopted, some people went to work dressed (or undressed) in tank tops and cutoffs. Just as those people were regarded as less than professionally attired (and perhaps less than professional), your message will be considered less important (and less than professional) if you choose a style that doesn't fit your corporate personality.

If you sell for a traditional luxury hotel company and you're selling to affluent baby boomers, for instance, your word choices, though conversational, should lean toward business formal (yet not be fake or pompous). You can show spirit, spunk, and your unique style while holding off on word choices that might seem too casual. A positive tone and correct word usage will provide the distraction-free reading zone that this type of prospect expects from you and your company. Consider yourself all suited up to play.

If you represent the same hotel (or product type), and your market is Gen X or Gen Y, you have more leeway. Don't be tempted, though, by those unbecoming cutoffs. Your company's reputation is on the line with every e-message you send. Both internal and external messages are filed and forwarded and reflect your professionalism, your concern, and your attention to detail. Your jacket may be at home, but your khaki pants are pressed and your shirt has a collar.

Still, one hotel company I work with is known for its quirkiness and playful sense. Let that shine in your e-mail messages—all the while keeping in mind that your job is to help the reader feel comfortable and confident with you and your product.

◆ ◆ ◆

You want to give your recipient the feeling that he knows you. Help him get to know your best side!

Match your writing voice with your e-mail purpose, too. Consider the message as much as your relationship with the client. For example, when you have a less than happy message (for example, the client's order is delayed or disrupted), even if you consider yourself good friends with the client, you probably don't want to begin with "Hey there!" In fact, don't even e-mail. You'll be much safer picking up the phone and talking to your friend/client because you'll naturally adjust your tone to hers and her level of concern during the conversation.

Finally, have confidence that *your* voice is good enough. It's you, and you are good enough! Don't imitate others. Smarter Biz wrote a wonderful blog post with the title "You Aren't Seth (Godin), Steve (Jobs), or (Robert) Scoble." The title seems to say it all, but it's still worth reading.

Be Brief

Franklin D. Roosevelt, the thirty-second president of the United States, gave the following advice: "Instructions for making a speech: Be sincere; be brief; be seated." Whether your presentation is verbal or through e-mail, that's still darn good advice.

You don't, however, need to send Twitter-ized messages or try to live up to Guy Kawasaki's blog suggestion that you never exceed five sentences when writing an e-mail. Five sentences *is* an awesome generalized concept. (See Guy's post: The Effective Emailer, February 3, 2006.)

Here's what you can do to be brief:

- If it doesn't matter to them, leave it out.
- If they aren't going to read it anyway, leave it out.
- If you've already said it or they already know it, leave it out.

When I was in college, a professor would turn back our reports and hand us colored pens (to avoid cheating). She would then require us to delete a specified number of words. We could leave class only when we had completed the task. You can imagine how quickly we learned to cut the clutter! (See, I nearly said cut *out* the clutter.)

Posting tweets on Twitter has been a great reinforcement to that college learning. When your reader expects your message to be fully contained within 140 characters, you (learn to) cut (out) (the) fluff and say it crisply. Make a sales proposal house rule: during the check step, eliminate X number of words. You'll tighten your message and earn respect from your recipient.

Is It a Dialogue or a Monologue?

Help your reader interact with your e-mail. Until your recipient responds to your message, e-mail is just a monologue. Just as great blog posts provide links to other relevant information, you can do the same. Hyperlink to your Web site or to other valuable content. And since most people today understand that a hyperlink (or link) can itself be clicked, there is no need to preface the link with, "Please click here."

Keep in mind, also, that most readers are intentional; they are on a mission to get to the information that matters to them. The easier and more intuitive you make it for them to find what they need, the more they'll like you, and the more they'll like doing business with you.

Is It Relevant and Compelling?

Offer valuable information. Provide content that the reader can't easily access elsewhere.

Back in the day, prospective customers actually needed a salesperson to provide them with basic facts and product features. Today, prospects can discover almost everything they need to know through a quick word search. Social media hasn't just changed how we write, it's changed what we write.

◆◆◆

There are only two reasons for a buyer to read your sales message. Your e-mail can

- Personalize and filter the content that exists on your Web site, or
- Help him feel safe and smart buying from you.

The plethora of information on the Web can easily overwhelm buyers. Smart salespeople see this overabundance of information as their golden ticket. They understand the paradox of too much information: that it leads to indecision. Buyers who aren't confident in their choices either don't make them or make the wrong ones (to go with your competitor, for instance). Use your e-mails to help them make sense of the information flow.

Successful salespeople (you!) must filter the overwhelming amount of content (even from your own company's Web site!) into a relevant, concise, authentic e-mail message. A powerful sales e-mail connects the dots between the outcome that the buyer needs and the sales solution that is being offered to help the reader feel confident and smart about his decision.

Is It Authentic?

Perhaps the biggest lesson learned about writing from social media is this: don't lie. Say only what you mean, and mean what you say. If you overpromise and underdeliver, everyone will know.

———————————————◆◆◆———————————————

Remember the "tattletale" in school? Social media is the ultimate player.

———————————————————————————————————

Tell true (short) stories in your e-mail about how customers have been helped by your products and services. If you can't tell the story crisply in just a few words, provide the link. (For instance, you might say: "one of the chief concerns customers have is whether we can deliver on time." You can easily link the words *chief concerns* with a story about a specific customer who doubted that you could deliver, and was delighted that you did. Or, you might link the words *deliver on time* to customer stories about how you successfully delivered on time.) Be transparent with your stories by not just saying, for instance, "a recent customer," but providing the customer's name and company title. (Get permission first.)

USE SOCIAL MEDIA TO ENGAGE YOUR CUSTOMERS

Personalization is king today, and social media helps you better understand your prospect's likes and dislikes. Beyond participating in LinkedIn discussions, Twitter, Facebook, and Foursquare, you can learn more about your customers, their business needs, and their initiatives with a simple, free service like Google alerts (www.google.com /alerts). You can read about what annoys customers at sites like Groubal.com. The more you know about what matters to your customers, the more you can create e-mails that go straight to the issues that resonate for them. "Join the conversation" isn't just a slogan, it's a way of life.

PART THREE

◆◆◆

SUCCESSFUL PROSPECTING WITH E-MAIL

If you keep on saying things are going to be bad,
you have a good chance of being a prophet.

—Isaac Bashevis Singer

Everyone is in business development today. Uncovering new business, whether from a cold and obscure source, a warm lead, or a former or current customer, is the second most profitable thing a salesperson can do. (The first most profitable? Taking good care of your existing customers.)

Yet for many sales professionals, even those with experience and excellent track records, prospecting or cold calling is uncomfortable and unsettling. Many hide behind e-mail with less than stellar results.

E-mail can be a highly profitable method of prospecting. It takes knowing what to write to engage a prospective buyer who may or may not be familiar with your product or service—or even care that your company exists.

This section provides the word tracks and tools you need to ensure that your prospecting messages begin trusting, profitable sales relationships.

CHAPTER 9

◆ ◆ ◆

WRITE "COLD E-MAIL" MESSAGES THAT GET RESULTS

The first step is the hardest: you need to care enough about the outcome that you're willing to call out the resistance, to stand up and shout it down.

—SETH GODIN

Writing a "cold" e-mail can be as awkward as making a cold telephone call or stopping in at a prospect's office without an appointment. An overly dramatic e-mail subject line, for instance, can arouse as much suspicion as a telemarketer who gets on the phone, botches the pronunciation of your name, and then asks, "How are you today?"

The key to successful cold e-mailing is authenticity. Just as a cold caller will have a better chance of engaging you if she can authentically bond with you, a cold e-mail will be more likely to be read if you have an authentic touchpoint. This touchpoint, or common bond, isn't always readily apparent, and it's critical to getting your e-mail read.

Using varied and realistic prospecting scenarios, we'll cover how to articulate your touchpoint in a way that engages your prospect and sets the tone for a meaningful and productive sales conversation.

FIRST, THE STRATEGY

As discussed in previous chapters, it's crucial that you know your purpose and selling strategy before you write. When prospecting, the first question, even before the planning questions, is simply to ask yourself: is e-mail the best tool to use? If it is, then determining your answers to the five planning questions will guide your success

Here is a scenario: Client A (we'll call her Maya) was thrilled with the excellence of your widgets. She loved your product and your service delivery. One day you get an e-mail from her, and she writes, "I have a great referral for you. Call my friend Parker at 555-555-5555; his e-mail is Parker@Parker.com. He'll love your widgets." Being the high-achieving sales professional that you are, before contacting her lead, you first follow up the referral with her. You ask her why she thinks Parker would be such a great lead. Her response: "He uses widgets like yours all the time, and I know he was really unhappy with the company he had been using. He may be using someone else by now (we haven't spoken in about a year), but I know he uses a lot of widgets. I'd call for you, but I'm swamped with this project I'm heading up. He's a good guy, though."

Armed with that information, you decide to e-mail him. You take the time to answer the prewriting questions to determine your sales strategy and writing purpose:

1. *Why?* To get Parker excited about how happy and successful he'll be if he uses your widgets.
2. *What?* Maya suggested that you might be looking for a reliable source for top-quality widgets.
3. *Accomplish?* Persuade Parker to take my call.
4. *Next step?* I phone Parker Thursday.
5. *Delighter?* Parker can relax, knowing that he'll enjoy an excellent product, great value, and excellent service delivery.

Because you've taken the time to plan your message, e-mail can be a smart way to prospect this referral. Your sales strategy isn't simply to send

Parker information saying you're "touching base" or asking him to follow up with you when he is ready to review his widget sourcing. Your strategy is to pique his interest enough, using Maya as the touchpoint, so that he sees the benefit of accepting your phone call. Your goal is to talk with Parker to determine if your widgets can help him create greater success.

YOU'VE BEEN REFERRED TO YOUR PROSPECT. WHAT DO YOU WRITE?

A referral is a relatively easy prospecting e-mail to write. It's a warm lead, and you have an easy, authentic, common bond: the person you both know. No matter how tenuous this bond is (new hire workshop attendees have suggested that I contact their CEO!), use it. Begin with the referrer's name, both in the subject line and in your first sentence.

The key to writing a great prospecting e-mail is this: speak the truth. At this point, you know you have two truths:

- Someone whom you both know referred you.
- You want to help the prospect create greater success.

Be authentic. Tell the prospect your truth.

Your e-mail might sound like this:

```
Subject: Maya Golden suggested I contact you

Hi Parker,

Maya suggested I contact you. She told me that you
use widgets frequently and might be looking for a
reliable supplier of high-quality product. She has
been delighted with both the service and the quality
of the products she has ordered from us, and she has
been delighted with the minimal 0.1 percent return rate
(almost unheard of in this industry!). I'll call you
```

```
Friday to talk about how you can count on a consistent
supply of top-quality widgets at a reasonable cost.
```

This e-mail is authentic, explaining to the prospect exactly what gives you the right to contact him and how he might be helped by what you have to offer. You've taken control of the next step and are clear about what that next step is. The message is clear, concise, and customer-centric.

You may be wondering whether the e-mail would be stronger if you indicated a specific time when you'd phone Parker ("I'll call you Wednesday at 1 p.m."). Although some sales trainers present this as a way for you to show reliability as well as to enable control, I recommend allowing yourself more room for error. Once you say that you'll call at a precise time, you have only 60 seconds to get it right. Too many things can get in the way of those 60 seconds. Perhaps another customer called you 10 minutes before your designated prospecting call time, and after much friendly banter, she has asked you to check availability for 10,000 widgets. Surely you aren't going to get off the phone. ("Oh, excuse me. Hold that thought. I just need to make this prospecting call, even though you're asking for business now.")

If you stay on the phone (which I certainly would recommend!) and call the prospect after 1 p.m., you have to begin with an apology ("I am so sorry I'm late")—never a great way to start.

If you'd like to be more specific than just providing the day or date, offer a time frame such as Wednesday *morning* or Wednesday *afternoon*. You give yourself much better odds of getting it right when you build in a swath of three to four hours.

Returning to the prospecting e-mail to Parker, did you notice how easy it was to speak your truth and move toward achieving your purpose? Here is the pattern:

- Start with a truthful touchpoint.
- Provide your solution in terms of the prospect.

- Explain the next step.
- Use the delighter to remind the prospect what is in it for him.

NO REFERRAL, BUT YOU HAVE SOMETHING IN COMMON WITH THE PROSPECT

The rules for writing a great prospecting e-mail stay the same whether you have a meaningful touchpoint (Maya's recommendation) or another less significant bond. It's still important to begin with how or why you know the prospect for two reasons: by providing the common bond, you answer her unasked questions (how do I know you and why should I interrupt my day to talk to you?), and by doing so, you earn the right to advance the conversation. If you share membership in an association, tell him right away. If you belong to the same health club, LinkedIn group, or professional association, tell her. If your kids go to the same school, martial arts class, or orthodontist, use this information as your common touchpoint, and as an attention-getting subject line.

Here is another situation: you belong to the same industry association as Abby. You've never met, but after a search of her company's Web site, you believe that she has a need for widgets.

Again, let's look at the purpose for writing:

1. *Why?* To get Abby excited about saving money with your widgets.
2. *What?* You, Abby, might be looking to save money on widgets.
3. *Accomplish?* Persuade her to let you know if she has a need for widgets.
4. *Next step?* She e-mails back saying that she uses widgets.
5. *Delighter?* You'll save time and money with ABC Widgets.

Abby uses widgets, but she is constantly bombarded by vendors who are trying to sell her on buying their widgets. Typically, she receives e-mails that say something like this:

```
Subject: Best Widgets in the World—10% off through
Thursday

Hi,

If you're looking for the best widgets in the world,
through Thursday, you can save 10%. These widgets
are made from wind, earth, and fire and can be used
whether the temperature is -5ºC or +30ºC. Widgets
come in blue, brown, black, and every other color
that begins with the letter B. Our widgets come
in sizes ranging from 1 to 1,000. Orders for sizes
larger than 5 are special orders and will not
receive this special pricing.

Thank you for your interest in widgets.
```

Let's step back to see what is wrong with that sales e-mail.

1. No touchpoint.
2. TMI. (Way too much information. Does she need to know the components of the widgets? If she only has an office in Arizona, does she need to know the low degree point? If she needs this information, could a hyperlink to specifications have been provided or a PDF attached?)
3. Bait and switch. Only a tiny percentage of widgets are actually on special.
4. There is no next step in the buying or sales process (other than the urgency to order before Thursday).

This e-mail is the type that salespeople send when they are hopeful that if they bomb and blast enough, surely some percentage of the people they send to will come back with orders. This isn't selling.

Here is an e-mail that begins with a touchpoint (notice the subject line), is truthful, focuses on the buyer, and accomplishes the writing goals:

```
Subject: XYZ Association colleague requests favor

Hi Abby,

I'm wondering if I can ask you a favor. May I
phone you next week? Our XYZ membership directory
shows that you are with the LMN Company, and after
researching LMN, it seems to me that you may have
a need for widgets. We may have a solution that
saves you money, but I want to be sure we really can
help. I'm in the office every day next week, except
Wednesday. If you'll e-mail me with a convenient time
for you, I'll call you to see if we can provide value
and save you time, too.
```

Forget the old-school push, push, push selling strategies. It's not "He who speaks fastest to the most people wins" but "He who thinks most about the other person wins."

Do you agree that this e-mail would be more likely to get opened, get read, and engage the buyer?

Did you notice that the opening of the sales message asks for a favor? Because you truly have a common bond (shared membership in an organization), it's highly likely that the other person will agree to the favor. If she doesn't respond to your request, it most likely means that she is busy, this isn't a good time, or she isn't interested. You can always follow up a few months later, again, with your truth:

```
Subject: XYZ Association colleague requests favor

Hi Abby,

I don't want to be a pest to you, and I'm wondering
if I can ask you a favor. May I phone you next week?
Our XYZ membership directory shows that you are
```

```
with the LMN Company, and after researching LMN, it
seems to me that you may have a need for widgets. We
may have a solution that saves you money. If you'll
e-mail me with a time that is convenient for you,
I'll call you to see if we can help you save money
and time.
```

YOU'VE DONE BUSINESS BEFORE—
MANY, MANY MOONS AGO

Once again, the pattern for writing a great prospecting e-mail stays the same.

- Start with a truthful touchpoint.
- Provide your solution in terms of the prospect.
- Explain the next step.
- Use the delighter to remind the prospect what is in it for him.

Applying this pattern requites a clear understanding of your sales strategy and the truth. You'll want to create an e-mail that is conversational, authentic, and focused on how the prospect will benefit.

Try your skill with this scenario. Your company recently underwent a major redistribution of sales territories. You are now working with a new market, in a new part of the world. The database you've been given is filled with the names of people who have done business with your company, but you are totally dependent on the notes of the salesperson who previously worked with them for any history. Some customers have no notes attached (surprise, surprise, surprise). Your mandate is to renew relationships with these former customers, based on whatever you know. Now what?

Looking through the database, you note that Lily was the planner for a meeting at your hotel in 2010.

You'll quickly gain control of the situation by answering the sales planning questions:

1. *Why?* To get Lily excited about how successful her meeting can be at ABC Hotel.
2. *What?* Your next meeting will be even more successful (productive, fun, memorable, better value) than when you met here in 2010.
3. *Accomplish?* Motivate Lily, the former customer, to take my call and start a trusting relationship with me.
4. *Next step?* I call her Friday.
5. *Delighter?* Her attendees will be excited by the value of ABC Hotel.

How will you write this e-mail to achieve your goals? Let the simple truth guide you. (We'll work on the subject line in a later chapter.)

Here are some truthful options to consider as your opening statement:

- Wait until your attendees return to the ABC Hotel!
- Welcome back to the ABC Hotel!
- Your next meeting will be even better than your last at the ABC Hotel.

◆◆◆

What is your truth? Open your sales message with it.

Depending on your personality, writing style, and company culture, you might move directly from that opening statement to your action statement. I prefer adding another sentence that supports my first statement claim.

Here is my e-mail:

```
Hi Lily,

Wait until your attendees return to the ABC Hotel!
They'll enjoy excellent value and be welcomed back by
```

```
a team that's dedicated to their success. I'll phone
you Friday to see how we can once again help you
achieve your meeting goals.
```

As in the other prospecting e-mails we've looked at, you started with your truth—a touchpoint that answers the immediate question your reader has: why is this person writing to me? You quickly provided your solution, explained the next step, and provided your "delighter."

WHEN YOU DON'T KNOW YOUR PROSPECT AND HE DOESN'T KNOW YOU (AND MAYBE DOESN'T EVEN CARE ABOUT YOU)

By now you've probably noticed that prospecting by e-mail is easy when it's genuine. Begin with your touchpoint: how you know the prospect or what the two of you have in common. Next, explain briefly what's in it for the prospect. Ask for the next step and close with a delighter—a benefit or reason that resonates for the buyer.

Here is another example to help you practice your prospecting skills. Your company is in desperate need of business. Your general manager decides that everyone must make five prospecting calls a day and send out a minimum of ten prospecting e-mails. To help you, she buys an address list of "qualified" prospects. She also suggests that you might want to use the phone book as a referral source.

One look at the "qualified" list and you know you're in trouble. You've been in sales long enough to know that the list is nothing more than names of people who *could* have a need for your service but may not.

Planning will give you the control you need to write a great sales message.

1. *Why?* To get them excited about how they might benefit from your service or product.

2. *What?* You'll never again have to do X; you can save time with Y; you can look good, feel smart, have hope (or whatever is an appropriate benefit for your service or product).
3. *Accomplish?* Motivate them to contact you directly.
4. *Next step?* They click on your e-mail address to get more info.
5. *Delighter?* They'll accomplish X and Y and Z more quickly and confidently.

What genuine statement can you make to begin your e-mail?

I might begin with: "Your name was given to me because you plan meetings/purchase widgets/select travel partners/decide on health plan options/write blogs (fill in the blank)" or "As a meeting planner/widget buyer/travel wholesaler/health executive/blog writer (fill in the blank), making the best choice in meeting venues/widgets/travel partners/health care options/servers (fill in the blank) is likely to be important to you." This is my only truthful touchpoint, and it answers the recipients' unasked questions.

Before reading the following sample e-mail, write your prospecting e-mail. Remember, after your touchpoint, explain what's in it for the buyer. This earns you the right to advance to the next step: asking for action.

Here is my e-mail:

```
Hi Name,

Your name was given to me because you've ordered
coffee products online within the last year. If you
enjoy the freshest coffee, delivered to your door,
wait until you try ABC coffee. One sip and you'll
know you won't be spending money at those high-priced
coffee shops anymore! Please e-mail me today for more
information about enjoying the smoothest, richest,
and best value coffee available today. You'll know
you made a great choice with that first sip!
```

Over the top, you say? Too salesy? Possibly. The honesty at the outset ("Your name was given to me because you've ordered coffee products online within the last year") sets the stage for a persuasive, results-oriented sales message. It also shows the reader that you've done your homework and that not everyone is receiving this offer.

You may have noticed that every e-mail example requires a next step. The goal of most prospecting e-mails is to start a meaningful conversation, not to close business. Looking at the coffee example, however, had the sales strategy been to persuade your prospect to click and order, you could have accomplished that by replacing "Please e-mail me today" with "Place your order today."

Writing excellent prospecting e-mails, like all sales writing, requires determining your message's purpose, being authentic, and caring more about your buyer's success than about closing the sale. Focus on helping buyers create greater success, and prospecting—instead of something to fear—becomes the beginning of a profitable relationship for both you and your buyer.

CHAPTER 10

◆◆◆

CRAFT POWERFUL
SUBJECT LINES

*Any man who can drive safely while kissing a pretty girl is
simply not giving the kiss the attention it deserves.*

—ALBERT EINSTEIN

Are your customers paying about as much attention to your e-mails
as the guy who is kissing and driving is paying attention to the kiss?
No matter how exciting or well presented your e-mail might be, if your
reader doesn't pay attention to your message because of a dull or hyperactive subject line, he won't open the message, and you're left unfulfilled.

Think about how you determine which e-mails you'll read. Most of
us check the sender's name and the subject line. If they don't "speak to
us" (aren't relevant to our needs), it's an easy decision to delete them
or delay reading them.

According to research by the e-mail marketing company ExactTarget, there are five stages of viewing an e-mail:

1. Sender's name
2. Subject line
3. Preview pane (what can be seen without opening the message)

4. Opened e-mail (what can be seen without scrolling down)
5. Full e-mail

Most organizations have standardized their e-mail addresses. If you're an independent rep, however, be sure that your name and e-mail address look and sound professional. Don't lose people with an address like Imhot@College.com.

Your e-mail address may also eliminate your message if your customer has had a bad experience with your company or thinks she has no reason to hear from your company at this time. There's little you can do about this other than to write an awesome subject line, but even an amazing subject line may not save your message from the trash file. When your e-mail address reflects a brand with a great reputation, it builds trust in your reader's mind and increases the likelihood that your message will be considered worthy of opening.

Once you pass "Go" (your e-mail name and address are acceptable), the next obstacle to having your e-mail opened and read is the subject line. Is your subject line interesting to the prospect? If it promises too much, your e-mail is immediately thought of as spam and trashed. If it isn't relevant, there is no reason for him to bother to open the message. We each make nanosecond decisions on what is important enough to interrupt our day and use up our time.

If your subject line and your e-mail name are judged to be relevant, interesting, or important to the reader, your e-mail makes it to the next stage: your reader reads what she can see in her preview pane. Typically, the preview pane shows 4 to 15 words. If these first few words go in a different direction from what you promised in your subject line, your message will be deleted.

When the first words are meaningful to the reader and aligned with her expectations based on your name and subject line, she continues to the next step and actually opens your e-mail. But you haven't made it around the board yet, because at this point, there is still another test. Without scrolling, is the chunk of information on her screen compelling, clear, and relevant? Is it aligned with what you promised in your subject line? Yes? Yes! You are about to collect your game money because her next move will be to scroll through your e-mail to read your full message and, you hope, take the action you suggested.

◆◆◆

At each juncture, your reader makes a decision: to read or not to read.

Whew! All those viewing stages, and you can lose the prospect at any of them. Of course, these viewing stages happen within seconds and, like stopping when we see a red light, are done without much conscious thought. Readers (you and I) don't say, "Let me look at the sender's name; now the subject line; now the preview pane." Yet we make these snap judgments to weed out anything that may take up our time and not be worth it.

SUBJECT LINES BUILD TRUST

The "rules" about what should or shouldn't be included in a subject line are a moving target. Because spammers often abuse authentic attention-getting ideas, what was a powerful attention getter yesterday may be as appealing as old fish today.

There are two guidelines, however, that, when you apply them consistently, will ensure that you will have an easy time crafting winning subject lines that get your messages opened.

1. Do Not Trick Your Reader with Your Subject Line

Don't be dishonest. Not in your subject line (or anywhere). If you are, you can count on it backfiring.

I received an e-mail from a personal address, although it turned out to be a vendor who had exhibited at a trade show at a meeting where I was the keynote speaker. The subject line said: "About our dinner." I knew that she and I hadn't had dinner together, but looking at that subject line, I wondered, did I miss it? Or, did I agree to meet this person for an upcoming dinner and forgot about it and her? I was so concerned that I had messed up, based on the subject line, that I quickly read the words that showed on my iPhone. They said: "I am sorry we missed having dinner together while we both …"

I was a nervous wreck—my entire reputation ruined!—so I tapped on the screen to open her e-mail. It said:

```
Hello Sue,

I am sorry we missed having dinner together while we
both attended the SHC meeting. If you didn't stop by
our booth and find out what DogPoop does, here is a link
to our multimedia tour: fulllinktodogpoop.com.here.

Please let me know if you'd like further information
from DogPoop.

Thanks and Regards.
```

Trick me once, shame on you! Her dishonest subject line, combined with her self-centered approach (you didn't stop by my booth!) and her outdated language (multimedia tour?), told me everything I need to know to decide that I will never do business with DogPoop.

As bad as this subject line is, it isn't the worst ever. The worst one, mainly because so many people currently use it, is this: "Question for an Article." However, when you open the e-mail, it's a sales pitch for their product. Trickery may work to get your e-mail opened, but it simultaneously spoils your reputation and any chance of a trusting relationship or possibility of a sale.

The purpose of the subject line shouldn't be simply to get the message opened. It should build trust with your reader to help him feel comfortable moving to the next viewing phase. Don't stretch the truth, promise something the e-mail doesn't deliver, or deceive the reader.

◆◆◆

Make your subject line a truthful summary of what your e-mail is actually about.

2. Make It Relevant to Your Reader

Your prospect has dozens, if not hundreds, of e-mails vying for her attention, and your unsolicited message probably isn't going to be at the top of her list to read. But you can break through the clutter and beat out the competition with a subject line that quietly says, "If you don't open me, you may miss something important." (You won't use those words, of course!)

THE RIGHT SUBJECT LINES GET RESULTS

Subject lines are most critical in the sales process when you're prospecting and the recipient doesn't know you. Once a relationship exists, all it should take is your name (the first viewing stage) for your customer to know that your message will be worth opening and reading. Before you've built that relationship, however, your subject line is the key to profitable results.

Start by noticing the solicitation e-mails that you open and read. What was comfortable about the subject line? What word or words influenced you?

Next, look at newspaper front pages and magazine covers. Think about how you determine what you'll read. Your subject line needs to work as hard as a headline does to capture attention. Which articles catch your eye? What magazine offers call out to you? The more aware you are of what appeals to you, the easier it will be to create results-oriented subject lines.

Here are additional tips to consider:

- **Keep your subject line short.** Current research suggests a 50-character maximum for the subject line so that your reader can read the entire subject line. But even 50 characters can be too long for some mobile phones, resulting in your carefully composed 50-character subject line truncated to: "Greetings from hot . . . ." Keep it short and crisp.

The subject line tells the reader what the e-mail is about and why it's important to read, in 50 characters or less.

- Use key words to clue your reader quickly. Here are a few to consider:
  Action request:
  Meeting request:
  Conference call request:
  Question:
  You're invited:
      Follow these key words with a summary of your request or question.
- **Use numbers.** There is something about specific numbers that intrigues us.
  5 ways to lose weight while you sleep
  12 running shoes that look as good as they feel
  15 nursing homes to avoid
  6 ways your company may be destroying the environment
      When your e-mail is truly about five ways to lose weight while you sleep (and not about one way to do this—*your* diet aid), use your subject line to announce it. Be as specific as you can in your subject line about what to expect in your e-mail message.
- **Use thought-provoking questions.** Keep the questions open-ended (ask yes/no questions only when you have a 51 percent chance or better that your reader will go in the direction you

want), and make the answer important to the reader's success. Here are some examples for prospecting e-mails:

- Did you get your free software app? It's here. (Readers can download the free software from your e-mail.)
- What color makes the most green? (Intriguing. What color does? The e-mail needs to explain what color makes the most money.)
- How do I communicate with difficult coworkers? (Provide answers, not just a pitch for your latest Webinar.)
- Are you looking for business growth? (Start this e-mail with something like: "Here is how you can grow your business: . . .")
- Are your attendees registering for your next meeting? (This e-mail needs to provide answers for persuading my attendees to register.)

SUBJECT LINES THAT CONVERT LEADS FOR THE COMPETITION

Take a quick look through your trash file, and you'll see lots of sales messages that didn't cut it. Why did you delete them? In addition to what has already been discussed, there are several other reasons that prospects won't bother reading your message. Here is a list of don'ts:

- **Don't misspell** (*important* message for you; *impotent* message for you). How sad to lose your chance of a sale because a word in the subject line is misspelled. There is no excuse for this lack of attention to detail.
- **Don't shout by capitalizing every word.** (HOW WOULD YOU SPEND $100?) The exception to this point is this: when you have great news for a customer who you currently do business with. No one minds THANK YOU! or YOU'RE THE BEST! or CONGRATULATIONS ON YOUR PROMOTION! in all CAPS.

- **Don't use the prospect's name, particularly in all CAPS.**
  (SUE, have you registered yet?) Even if we're friends, don't shout
  my name to get my attention.
- **Don't leave out words** ("Need talk about order"). You're sending an e-mail, not a telegram. *Stop.* You do not need to omit
  words. *Stop.*
- **Don't leave the subject line blank.** This is just rude. It's bad
  enough that you're interrupting your prospect with your e-mail.
  Now you want him to guess what your message is about. One
  company I work with feels so strongly about this that it has told its
  associates that they are not responsible for opening e-mails from
  each other unless the subject line field is completed. (Yes, they
  do open them from their customers!) This direction came about
  to avoid behavior that was deemed as showing little compassion
  for other people's time.
- **Don't use your subject line as the beginning of the first line
  of your e-mail,** expecting your reader to connect the subject line
  phrase with the opening line of the e-mail. Here is an example:

```
Subject line: 40% off today if you mention code . . .

PROMO. This special offer for our best customers
gives you huge savings and is only good today . . .
```

   Rather than confuse readers, think of the subject line only as
a headline and not as a sentence starter. Save the ellipses (. . .) for
your more literary work when you want to let your reader know
that you've chosen to leave the sentence incomplete so that he
can ponder.

   When your entire message fits in your subject line, however,
you can write it in the subject line but beware: many people
find this technique annoying. If your customer is waiting to hear
if you can ship his order before November 14, you can write:
"Nov. 12 shipment confirmed." If you choose to do this, add a
signal to your reader that this is the full message. Common sig-

nals are <EOM> (end of message) and <SLO> (single line only). Because <SLO> can be easily confused with SOL (shucks out of luck), I recommend using <EOM> instead!

- **Don't use only one word.** Imagine that you've just had a great phone conversation with your customer, and you promise to send the link to the article that you talked about. You locate the link and are tempted to e-mail it with the subject line: *Link*. Don't do it. Take the extra moment to describe what you're sending. It will be easier for both of you to find it again, file it, and forward it. Try: *Link: Lost Farm Golf Club.*

HELP THEM WANT TO OPEN YOUR SALES MESSAGE

What subject lines would you write for the e-mails discussed in Chapter 9? What can you say that is simple and truthful to influence your recipient to read this e-mail?

```
Hi Lily,

Wait until your attendees return to the ABC Hotel!
They'll enjoy excellent value and be welcomed back by
a team that's dedicated to their success. I'll phone
you Friday to see how we can help you achieve your
meeting goals.
```

Possible subject lines might be

- Welcome back to the ABC Hotel
- Enjoy excellent value and be served by professionals
- May we help you achieve your meeting goals?
- Action request: phone call Friday

What about when you have no history with the prospect? What subject line would you create for this selling message?

```
Hi Name,

Your name was given to me because you've ordered
coffee products online within the last year. If you
enjoy the freshest coffee, delivered to your door,
wait until you try ABC coffee. One sip and you'll
know you won't be spending money at those high-priced
coffee shops anymore! Please e-mail me today for more
information about enjoying the smoothest, richest,
and best value coffee available today. You'll know
you made a great choice with that first sip!
```

Possible subject lines might be

- Fresh coffee delivered to your door
- What is a great sip of coffee worth?
- Home-delivered coffee for you to savor
- Save time and money with fresh, rich coffee delivered

The goal of your subject line is to pique the reader's interest and persuade her to open, read, and act on your e-mail. This is accomplished by creating a headline that is authentic, interesting, and likable. The more trustworthy you sound, the more likely your reader will be to trust you with her time, attention, and money.

CHAPTER 11

◆ ◆ ◆

ASK FOR WHAT YOU WANT—
AND GET IT!

*The minute you settle for less than you deserve, you get
even less than you settled for.*

—MAUREEN DOWD

If I had one dollar for every e-mail, "sales" letter, or proposal I've
received that did not close with a clear, powerful action step, I'd be
on my yacht with a martini (stirred, not shaken) in hand, waiting for
my helicopter to transport me to my private Gulfstream G550 to jet
me to my villa mountain retreat, where a team of butlers would have
my bath drawn and my 1907 Piper-Heidsieck champagne chilling.

An impactful, clear closing statement motivates your reader to act.
A poorly written (or nonexistent) close is like an Olympic gymnast
who falls on dismounting. No matter how perfectly executed the rest
of her program was, important points are deducted that might cause
a medal loss. Likewise, your e-mail can be genuine and compelling,
but if it doesn't clarify the next step, you lose virtual points, and you
also might lose the sale. This should never happen.

Consider these closing statements. Are they clear, persuasive, and
action-oriented?

- "If I can be of further assistance, please do not hesitate to call."
- "I'll phone you to talk about how we can work together."
- "Thanks again for your interest."
- "Please review."
- "What do you think?"
- "Please feel free to contact me should you have any questions."

Those statements give me gas! They don't tell the reader anything he doesn't already know, aren't specific, and don't ask for or describe a clear next step.

Unless you're writing only, purely, and single-mindedly to disseminate information, without the need for a reply or another forward action (and this would be atypical for sales professionals because every interaction with a customer should move toward another next step), a precise, easy-to-follow action step is mandatory. Consider this as a writing commandment: honor thy action step!

◆ ◆ ◆

To ensure that your sales letter is powerful, be relentless about including a clear, easy-to-understand action step.

Define the action that *you* will take next ("I'll phone you Tuesday morning"; "I'll follow up with you after your executive meeting"; "I'll text you when I'm on my way to the meeting room") or explain the action that you would like them to take ("Please complete the order form with the number of widgets to be shipped to your Auckland office and …").

As previously mentioned, savvy sales reps know that it's best to maintain control of the next step. Once you ask the other person to take that next step, you become dependent on him to do it. If he doesn't follow up with you, then what? You'll have to work even harder to regain his attention.

Circumstances exist, however, in which it's appropriate for the prospect to be required to take the next step, and we've looked at some of them already. Recall the situation where you had a number of options to offer your customer. It wasn't your place to select the best option (none of them precisely fit her needs). Instead, the e-mail offered to follow up as she suggested: "What will work best? Please let me know which option is best for you, or if you have another idea, and I'll follow through as soon as I receive your e-mail."

There are other times when the writer deliberately wants to put the burden of responsibility on the reader. Most often, however, not only are you, the sales professional, obliged to take the next step, but you want and desire the opportunity to control that next step. No matter who has to do it, though, it must be clear that someone has to do something.

The salesperson who wrote the following e-mail took the time to respond to his lead. But now what? What is the reader supposed to do next? What can the writer expect to happen now?

```
Good Afternoon, Sophie:

Thank you for the opportunity to be considered
as your 2012 primary vendor! I've attached the
information you requested. If you have any questions,
please do not hesitate to phone me direct.

Thank you for your time and consideration. We look
forward to a positive response.
```

How will this sale move forward? Is the statement, "If you have any questions, please do not hesitate to phone me direct," supposed to be an action request? Or is the last sentence, "We look forward to a positive response," intended to motivate Sophie to act? What is "a positive response" to this e-mail, anyway? Should Sophie e-mail back, "Okay"? The action statement has gone missing!

Determining the next step requires you to consider your sales and writing strategy. Is the salesperson's point to say, "Here is the information; we're excited, and our fingers are crossed that you'll pick us"? Or, does he want to use the opportunity he has been handed to sell his company as Sophie's vendor of choice? Planning for the desired outcome, of course, is the first step:

1. *Why?* To let Sophie know that she can depend on my company's expertise to meet her distribution needs.
2. *What?* You, Sophie, can count on our outstanding record of reliability to ensure the success of your project.
3. *Accomplish?* To start a trusting relationship and persuade Sophie to send more details or take my call.
4. *Next step?* Sophie completes the RFP and e-mails it back or accepts my phone call to discuss her needs.
5. *Delighter?* She can feel confident that her distribution needs will be handled with excellence.

Here is a rewrite of that e-mail:

Subject: Follow-up to your request: Distribution qualification

Good afternoon, Sophie,

Thank you for considering ABC as a partner in your success! We are qualified vendors with an extensive track record of reliability, creating award-winning designs on time. Here are case studies, client testimonials, and documentation of our LEED certification and our other sustainability initiatives.

I've attached an RFP and will phone you Thursday afternoon to review your needs. We can quickly walk through the RFP while on the phone if you don't have a chance to complete it before we talk.

Thank you again for contacting ABC. You can count on us to handle your distribution needs with excellence.

Because Sophie requested the information, there is no need to be concerned with an attention-getting headline to this message. Sophie is already paying attention, but she may need to be reminded that you are following up on *her* request, rather than cold calling for her business. This sales message is smart to begin with the main idea (the answer to Sophie's question). The focus is on the reader's needs. The clear call for action ("I'll phone you Thursday"), the focus on the benefits to Sophie, and the delighter ("You can count on us to handle your distribution needs with excellence") turn a "telling" message into a "selling" one.

The underlined words in the e-mail are hyperlinks to the appropriate information. The writer saves Sophie time, filtering out nonessential information and pointing her in the direction that will help her feel safe and smart in making her purchasing decision.

◆◆◆

A clear, powerful action statement is the only way to move the reader to take action.

The first part of a powerful action step is ensuring there is one. When the reader finishes reading your email, he should know exactly who is going to take the next step.

Action steps should also provide a rationale for the reader to accept or take the action. Here is that list of poor closings from earlier in the chapter and suggested revisions. Notice how each action step is clear about who is responsible for taking the next step and also provides a reason to take it.

- Instead of: "If I can be of further assistance, please do not hesitate to call."
  Try: I'll call you tomorrow afternoon to confirm you received the widgets and to ensure they exactly meet your needs.
- Instead of: "I'll phone you to talk about how we can work together."

Try: I'll phone you Wednesday morning to discuss exciting, new options for your best meeting ever!

- Instead of: "Thanks again for your interest." (No action required)
  Try: You've made a great choice!
- Instead of: "Please review."
  Try: I'll call you Friday to answer any questions that may have come up during your review of the proposal and to ensure you have everything you need for a memorable and fun event.
- Instead of: "What do you think?"
  Try: As soon as you e-mail me with your preferred option, I'll move forward accordingly.
- Instead of: "Please feel free to contact me should you have any questions."
  Try: I'll call you Monday to ensure everything is running smoothly for you.

SOME SAY IT WON'T FLY

Earlier in this book we talked about being careful not to overpromise and underdeliver by telling a prospect you would phone at an exact time. As mentioned, it's quite easy for that promised time to come and go with the call not placed. On the opposite end of the spectrum, some workshop participants claim that they can't even include a specific date. They tell me that they have little control over their day, so they are afraid to commit to a precise date to phone the prospect.

It's true that we all have days that spin out of control. The car breaks down, and when, after waiting for help, we're finally on our way, the front tire blows, and while we're changing the tire, we get grease on the perfect business casual attire we chose to wear to make our presentation at the staff meeting, and so we have to stop at the mall to pick up new slacks and a shirt or blouse to match, and we arrive at the staff meeting only to discover that the original agenda has been sacked and replaced by the regional director's surprise visit and her desire for an overview of the team's sales goals, which were due next week, today, and so we have to excuse ourselves to work on our goals and slide deck. Those promised phone calls probably won't get made that day.

We've all canceled appointments and missed meetings, we've been late for our kids, and we've missed flights, but for the most part, when we plan to do something, we do it. Failing to plan, however, is planning to fail.

What is the use of writing a fabulous business letter and then not fabulously following up? Why lose the opportunity to showcase your responsiveness and attention to detail by following up when it suits your fancy, "within the next two weeks," or "next month," or worse, not mentioning it all?

Use your database to remind you when to call. Check your calendar and schedule the date you'll follow up with the client. Plan it and do it. You'll own the competitive edge, and you'll show your customer how responsive and trustworthy (and maybe even likable!) you are.

What if the day you choose is one of those days that totally goes wacky?

When your day spins out of control, call the prospect the next morning, or as soon as you are able. He probably wasn't waiting to exhale until you phoned. Don't make a big deal out of your delay. Say something friendly, like, "Good morning, Everett. Yesterday got away from me, and I had promised to phone you. Is this a good time to talk about your . . . ?" Try not to begin with a profuse apology. You'll still win points (enough to beat out the person who is calling sometime *within the next month!*) with your follow-through.

A race car driver once said that if you're going to win, you have to finish. Finish your sales e-mail by making the next step clear and easy to accomplish. Follow up like the professional you are. You'll be in the winner's circle in no time!

CHAPTER 12

◆ ◆ ◆

BUILD INTEREST TO SELL MORE EASILY

*Your purpose is to make your audience see what you saw,
hear what you heard, feel what you felt. . . . Relevant detail,
couched in concrete, colorful language, is the best way to recreate
the incident as it happened and to picturize it for the audience.*

—MARK TWAIN

You've written a subject line that commands attention because it is simple, truthful, and relevant. Your prospect clicks on your message, hopeful that he'll read something meaningful but aware that the subject line may be a ruse. He's ready to delete at a nanosecond's notice.

You have his attention—build on it. Help him visualize his success. Get him excited with your words! Titillate his senses with sensory, emotion-laden words. Tell brief, truthful stories. The more sensory your words, while still maintaining brevity, the more your reader will respond.

KEY WORDS INFLUENCE CUSTOMERS

Buyers respond to different stimuli. The three main types of stimuli, or styles in which people communicate and understand information, are visual, auditory, and kinesthetic. Visual learners learn by seeing. They like to read and are quick to see the meaning of the words on the page. You enhance their reading pleasure by using words that are full of imagery, helping them to visualize word pictures in their mind's eye easily.

Auditory learners prefer to hear what you have to say. They prefer hearing your voice on the phone to reading your words in your e-mail (a great reason to use the phone as well as e-mail). To keep them listening to your e-mail message, it's important to use "hearing" words. (Notice the use of the word *listening* in that sentence.) Words that help them hear the explanation or emphasize what they hear (this idea *rings* with truth, let's *talk* through this) keep them reading (often aloud so that they can hear the words).

Kinesthetic learners rapidly connect with an idea or product that they can touch, sense, or feel. Words that are palpable help them to grasp, hold on to, explore, discover, and handle the message. They want to feel or sense how something is done.

Read these opening paragraphs from a fabulous sales letter written by Candace Taylor and Deborah Weiss. At the time they wrote this e-mail, they both worked for a resort in Tucson, Arizona. I've highlighted some of the visual (V), auditory (A), and kinesthetic (K) words for you.

As you read, notice how Candace and Deborah used their referral source to connect immediately in a truthful, transparent, and authentic way and create a touchpoint. Because they were responding to a request for proposal, they knew their reader was interested in hearing from them and learning more about what they had to offer. They didn't have to break through the reader's preoccupation, but they did have to beat out the 12, 21, or 121 competitors from whom the prospect may also have requested information. The e-mail is long, and you might be more comfortable eliminating some of their words. The sales message, however, is a wonderful example of engaging the buyer's senses.

```
Hi Mr. Michaels,

Presley Shayna at the Metropolitan Tucson Convention
and Visitors Bureau tells us you're considering
```

Tucson as a site for your ABC meeting. That's great news! Now just imagine (K) this:

- From the moment your guests arrive at the ABC Resort, they'll know you've chosen someplace very special for them. Three-story-high windows (V) and majestic mountain views (V) will wow (K) them as they walk (K) into the comfortably elegant lobby. They will appreciate the spacious lobby lounge and welcoming conversational areas, perfect for networking and visiting, an important aspect of any gathering.

- Nothing beats a good night's sleep, and you can rest assured that your participants will be warm (K) and comfortable in our luxurious (K) guestrooms with the distinctive ABC Beds and ABC Bath products. Guests can experience (K) the beauty of a Tucson sunrise or sunset from their private balcony or patio. (V)

- You'll be holding (K) your program in meeting space that has been designed by planners just like you, with an eye for detail (V) and an emphasis on natural light, flexibility, and lots of breakout options. Your attendees will be able to enjoy the beautiful views and Tucson's 320 days of annual sunshine from the lovely terraces, patios, and outdoor venues.

- Picture (V) the fun and camaraderie your attendees will have playing a golf course designed by Jack Nicklaus himself, or the refreshed and rejuvenated spirits (K) they'll have after a day at the ABC Spa. Or, how about the total relaxation (K) they'll have enjoying the best pool area in Tucson (with a

swim-up bar, adult pool, and waterslide), or their
delight in finding (K) a perfect Tucson treasure
(V) in one of our boutiques. To throw some
adventure (K) into your program, just imagine (V)
them heading off for desert jeep rides, mountain
biking, hiking, or even a real-life cattle drive!

• You'll be hearing (A) rave reviews from attendees
who leave with rich memories of sunny skies,
soaring saguaro cacti, and a unique cultural
heritage. (V) This is the Arizona they imagined. (K)

How could you *not* continue to read? (I'll bet you even want to
continue reading their letter now. You'll get to read more in the next
chapters.) The reader—any reader—can hear, see, and sense the Arizona desert and the benefits of the beautiful hotel through the writers'
words. Deborah and Candace began their message by being genuine
and compelled their prospect (and us!) to continue reading by connecting the dots between what they offer and what the customer needs
if he is to accomplish his meeting objectives. Features and benefits are
not thrown in simply because they exist. Everything is connected to
Mr. Michaels's success.

Once you influence your readers to pay attention to you, keep their
attention by varying word choices—not by using fancy words, but by
choosing words that titillate the five senses to create a more memorable, stronger sales message

TELL YOUR STORY

I can still remember as a kid watching a television advertisement
for an appliance store (Jamaica Gas & Electric, known as J.G.E.)
in which the owner, Jerry Rosenberg, would be asked by an off-
camera, highly New Yawk-ish accented voice, "What's the stooory,
Jerry?" Jerry would respond in an even stronger New York accent,

"That's the stoooooory." Recounting this famous (or infamous) conversation doesn't do the commercial justice because the accent has to be heard to be believed. (Think Andrew Cuomo, but more.) The expression "What's the story?" like "You had me at hello" or "Fuggedaboudit," quickly entered everyday conversation. Families and friends would greet each other with "What's the story?" and the other person would gladly oblige, usually with a telling of something odd, interesting, or humorous that had happened that day. Everyone has a story.

What's your story? Your customers want to know. They can find facts anywhere. What they need from you is the emotional bond that will set your product apart, be memorable, and make it worthwhile to argue your case when other stakeholders may favor options that don't include you.

Telling stories creates an emotional connection that is impossible to achieve by spouting facts. Customers expect you to know what you sell; they need you to help them want to buy it.

Situated on a beautiful lake in the Midwest, a hotel I consult with is surrounded by pristine beauty. The hotel itself is ready for a few planned updates, yet holding a meeting there would be an exciting and smart decision. Why? As beautiful as the location is, it isn't the surroundings that make selecting this hotel a smart choice, it's the people. When you meet the dedicated, experienced team of hard-working professionals who seem to innately care about their customers' happiness and delight, you know that they'll get it right and that your event will be a success. But the sales team was struggling to sell the concept of "you can depend on us to make you shine." Given their Midwestern values, it was uncomfortable for them to brag about their expertise and what they accomplish for others. Sadly, they settled on selling what every one of their competitors sells: space, dates, and rates in gorgeous surroundings.

By using stories, however, they found a way to brag about themselves and still be humble. They could highlight and identify their extraordinary abilities simply by recollecting what others said about them. I only had to contact a few of the hotel's customers to start hearing brag-worthy stories about the dedicated team. In response to my question, "Can you tell me about an experience at the hotel that stands out in your mind?" here is what I heard:

"Well, I still have people talking about the chariot races. Long story short, I needed a path around my attendees—a much larger group than was originally planned for—for our themed-night entrance of chariot riders. I have no idea how but they did it, they used their creativity and can-do attitude to create the perfect path for an unforgettable grand entrance. . . ."

"Their 'we will help you' attitude. It was amazing because the restaurant was packed with people, but when I asked my server about the wine room for a potential dinner, she offered to show it to me so I could see how it could be set up for my group. At first, I said no because I just felt sorry for her because she was so busy. But I could tell she was really proud of it, and *wanted* me to see it."

"We were using all their space and didn't know what to do when an important sponsor insisted they be allowed to host a formal private dinner. We knew there was no space left. When we asked the hotel if they could transform the sponsor's hospitality suite, which had a pool table and a large-screen TV in it, into a fine dining establishment for a dinner, we thought they'd be challenged, particularly because we were making all our requests at the last minute by conference call! They were amazing! The event was perfect, and the sponsor was thrilled. They are good people who make things happen right—no matter what the challenge."

These true stories easily overcome the tired bathroom fixtures! By incorporating your stories into your sales e-mails, you easily set yourself apart.

What types of stories are being told about your products, company, or brand? What types of stories are you telling?

USE STORIES TO ENGAGE BUYERS

Here is an example of how you can build interest by using a story to sell more. You've contacted a key prospect multiple times, and she has not responded. Though she has never replied, you know that she currently sources the X widget. The X widget is more expensive and less reliable, but it carries status in some circles. Your product, the Y widget, is made out of materials that are not as high end, and that is why it sells for significantly less. But in double-blind tests, the Y widget (your product) has performed better in every category (even with your cheaper materials)! With your new power sales writing skills, you decide to approach the prospect one more time. You know your product will save her company money and will be just as reliable. You pull up your last e-mail to her and it says:

```
Hi Hailey,

I've left several messages for you and haven't heard
back, so I thought you might respond to an e-mail. I
noticed that you currently buy X widgets, and I can
save you substantial amounts of money by switching
you to Y widgets. I'd like to stop by your office
to show you a demo and point out the differences
between the X and Y models. I think you'll find
that what you're paying for is the name more than
anything else. I know your financial people will be
very pleased with the cost savings and the product.
```

Right away, you can see several reasons why Hailey didn't bother to respond.

1. **The writer isn't very likable.** The first sentence, "I've left several messages for you and haven't heard back, so I thought you might respond to an e-mail," has the potential to make the reader feel

negligent (or worse) for not responding. Guilt is not a sustainable selling proposition! Also, by saying, "I think you'll find that what you're paying for is the name more than anything else," you may make the prospect feel stupid and shallow (which, of course, is never clever).

2. **The writer offers no next step.** He hints at what he'd like to have happen ("I'd like to stop by your office to show you a demo"), but he doesn't have an action step to get the appointment. With an e-mail like this, it's doubtful that the prospect will take the initiative and e-mail the writer to say, "Come on down, y'all."

3. **The writer has no clear purpose for writing.** Rather than using a plan–do–check strategy, the writer used the easy but ineffective no-thinking strategy.

Answering the planning—or thinking—questions might yield this:

1. *Why?* To excite her about the potential of providing her associates with the best product while she garners significant savings for her company.

2. *What?* Like so many widget buyers, you, too, might be surprised by the results of a recent double-blind research study that enables time and money savings on widgets

3. *Accomplish?* Persuade her to take my call.

4. *Next step?* I phone her Monday afternoon.

5. *Delighter?* She introduces her company to a product that will reduce costs and boost productivity, and she looks brilliant!

Here's a hint: What story can you tell her that will engage her and create a positive emotional bond? Take a few minutes to write your e-mail before reading the option I've provided.

```
Hi Hailey,

"When I saw the double-blind test results, I couldn't
believe it either!" That's exactly what Sam Smith
```

at ABC Products said when he read the research comparing X and Y widgets. "This can't be true!"

If you're like many of our new customers, you'll be surprised too. In double-blind tests, the Y widget outperformed the X widget in every category. If Y cost more, this news wouldn't be so surprising, but it actually costs significantly less, even without a bulk discount.

I'll phone you Monday afternoon to talk about the results that Sam and others have enjoyed. You can count on lower costs and higher productivity with the high-performance Y widget!

What does this e-mail do right?

1. It helps the reader feel safe and smart.
2. It builds emotional connection with the story.
3. It's focused on Hailey and not on the writer.
4. The action is clear.
5. The purpose is clear.

The story, "'When I saw the double-blind test results, I couldn't believe it either!' That's exactly what Sam Smith at ABC Products said when he read the research comparing X and Y widgets. 'This can't be true!'" draws the reader in, helping her feel comfortable reading further. The story grabs the prospect's attention, helps her feel okay about her previous choice, and moves her toward the next step: accepting your phone call on Monday.

The story offers emotional and irrefutable evidence that it is safe to buy. Attorneys call this "substantive proof" or "demonstrative evidence." Robert Cialdini, in his seminal book *Influence*, calls it "social proof." Whatever you call it, use it! When other people do it, buy it, like it, and want it, we, too, do it, buy it, like it, and want it. Let your prospects know how others feel about your product or service. Let them hear the words and stories that others use to describe your awesome service, your impeccable attention to detail, and your concern for their success. By recounting the words of a delighted client, you're extending your hand and inviting the buyer to buy rather than selling or "bragging."

◆◆◆

What feature do you have a hard time selling? Don't be dishonest. How do other customers use it? What was their positive experience? Tell their truthful success stories. Show growth from what they thought to what they now know.

A Boston hotel client received a thank you e-mail from a recent groom. Here it is in part, enough to tell the story: "Since a lot of the night seems a little (thank you, champagne!) foggy for us, we've been relying on the inundation of thank yous and recaps from our guests that we continue to receive each day that we've been back from Hawaii! The common theme of the comments is people telling us that our night *'was the best wedding EVER!!!'* Seriously! This is all we keep hearing from people!" Would you agree that not using this story when prospecting to brides and grooms would be a major mistake?

Let's say you've purchased a list of brides and grooms from a bridal fair. How can you use the groom's story to persuade them that they, too, will be delighted at your hotel? The first thing to do, of course, is plan your message:

1. *Why?* To excite them about the perfect wedding celebration.
2. *What?* Your wedding day dreams will come true, and you can count on meaningful lifelong memories.
3. *Accomplish?* Persuade them to contact me to see the hotel.
4. *Next step?* They e-mail me back with available meeting times.
5. *Delighter?* You can count on your friends saying, "This was the best wedding ever!"

Now, try your hand at writing an e-mail that will leave your competitors at the altar. Incorporate the story to set your sales message apart.

Hi Soon-to-be Bride and Groom (Names, of course),

"Since the night seems a little foggy for us (thank you, champagne!), we've been relying on the thank yous we've received each day since we've been back from Hawaii! The common theme is that our night 'was the best wedding EVER!!!' Seriously! This is all we keep hearing from people!" Buster Brown, December 5, 2011, ABC Hotel.

The ABC Hotel invites you to experience a wedding day that your friends will talk about forever! From your grand entrance as husband and wife to the perfect toast to life together, you'll love what the ABC can do to make your celebration unique and memorable.

Name, when you have a moment, please e-mail me with a time that is convenient for both of you to come visit the hotel. As soon as you walk through our doors, you'll know your friends will rave about your wedding, too.

Start your perfect life together with the best wedding ever!

Did you include the story about the champagne in your sales letter? Including the groom's parenthetical comment makes the story even more authentic and endearing. If the bride and groom hadn't been having so much fun, they wouldn't have been relying on their friends' comments. The quirkiness makes the story believable and should be included in your sales story. Delete unnecessary words, though (compare the differences between what the groom actually wrote and how it appears in the cold-call e-mail) to keep the message concise and punchy. Also, take the liberty to change words that are misused or misspelled to make the person providing the social proof look smart and to avoid embarrassing him. (The groom originally spelled champagne in a more creative way: champaign.) Your job is to make everyone look smart.

◆◆◆

The best way to talk about your features is for *you* not to talk about it at all. Tell stories from your delighted customers instead.

In thinking about the e-mail to the prospective brides and grooms, what subject line might you use? Although this is a business message from you, the recipients aren't likely to be thinking of their wedding celebration as a business proposition. This gives you more variety in how you can approach them, keeping within the guidelines previously mentioned.

How about:

- Champagne. Friends. Love.
- What will friends say about your wedding?
- We can't wait to receive your thank you. Seriously.

Use the words of your delighted customers to convince your prospects that you have what it takes to produce the tangible and intangible benefits you've promised.

Quotations from pleased buyers demonstrate evidence of acceptability and offer your readers ironclad social proof that you (your service or your product) will perform. Regardless of whether you sell wedding space, widgets, or whatever, it can be challenging to sell the product with as much enthusiasm and veracity as a customer's story does. Repeating a customer's experience adds credibility and aids salespeople who think they may be too pushy or in your face. Stories make it easier to authentically engage the buyer.

Word-of-mouth referral—the social proof inherent in the story—drives more revenue and greater profitability than any other method of selling. It's the simplest and easiest way to educate buyers about features. I can *say* that I'm the greatest speaker in the galaxy. (What else am I going to say—that I'm the worst?) Nothing I could say to prospective buyers, however, could be more effective than quoting what my clients actually say and the stories they tell about what happens after I leave. In sales e-mails, we often say: "Here's what your <u>colleagues</u> say about Sue."

Cialdini's principle of social proof is easy to use in e-mail. Find those complimentary letters you've archived, pull out the portion that highlights the qualities you want your prospect to remember, and start your e-mail with the testimonial. Let your satisfied buyers educate prospects about your product and its features. You'll get more accomplished with a story than with any seemingly biased description or explanation that you can provide.

◆ ◆ ◆

Let your buyers know that they have nothing to fear. Use social proof to make buying easy.

PART FOUR

◆◆◆

BRAND YOURSELF AS A PROFESSIONAL

Professional men (and women!), they have no cares;
whatever happens, they get theirs.

—Ogden Nash

Powerful writers get things done. Their sales messages move their buyers to act. Their e-mails and proposals, whether they're directed toward internal customers or toward external clients, get them the results they want.

The previous chapters in this book have taught you to start your sales messages with purposeful, truthful, and compelling statements that focus on the benefits your prospects will receive. By using stories and key words, you help your readers see, hear, and practically touch those benefits. This next step keeps the momentum going for you. It's the education step, and it's probably the step you've been waiting for. Like a woman in labor, now is the time you finally get to push . . . your brand! This is your opportunity to differentiate yourself by proving to your buyers that you get it; you understand their need to prove themselves and sell their decisions to their stakeholders. This is your chance to stand out, demonstrate your concern for detail, and earn the right to serve and service them. In this section, you'll read about ideas to extend and enhance your brand image and more easily sell more.

CHAPTER 13

◆◆◆

USE THE LANGUAGE OF BUSINESS TO DRIVE PROFITS

A brand is a set of differentiating promises that links a product to its customers.

—STUART AGRES

Even when you sell to the decision maker, you may not actually be selling to the decision maker. The power behind the throne can be deceiving.

Let's say that the meeting professional is responsible for selecting the meeting destination and venue, hiring speakers, and booking the off-site meeting activities. Let's also say that you sell for a hotel, are a speaker, or provide destination management services, team-building activities, or food, fun, or beverage options. You have connected with the ABC Corporation's meeting planner, and she seems interested in working with you. Your prices are competitive, your product is timely, and your service record is impeccable. But you don't book the business.

This all-too-common occurrence can happen when the salesperson becomes complacent, believing that he is communicating with the actual decision maker. Here is the ironic part: you are dealing with the decision maker, but if she can't sell her decision to her decision makers, you have no deal. Without the endorsement or support of the meeting professional's counterparts, committee, or executive team, it's likely that she will go in another direction.

Almost without exception (the exceptions being a one-person business, an entrepreneur, or a dictatorship), your decision maker needs or wants to persuade others that the choice he is making is smart and safe. Even the CEO of a large company, although certainly entitled to make a unilateral decision, may want to discuss options with a board or committee and seek approval from others.

The point of this discussion is this: the more you incorporate the language of business, understand your prospect's business initiatives, and take his stakeholders' needs into account, the more you can create a sales message that invites him to buy. When your decision maker can approach others with the information you've armed him with, you make it easy for the buying decision to fall in your favor.

Here is an example of a good e-mail, although it may not be good enough:

```
Hi Ethan,

Brian Matthew suggested I contact you. He told me
that you hold incentive meetings in fun destinations.
Your group will love this special, exclusive
destination! I'll call you Friday to talk about how
your attendees can be wowed by your selection of
sand, sun, and savings!
```

The writer smartly used Brian's name as a touchpoint to form a quick bond with the prospect, then explained what she had learned from Brian and why she was contacting Ethan. The hyperlink is clever because the writer provides the information without feature puking. Even the call for action is purposeful, clearly explaining what is in it for Ethan to take the call: "to talk about how your attendees can be wowed by your selection of sand, sun, and savings!"

This e-mail may not be enough to persuade the buyer, however, because it doesn't incorporate the language of business. How will Ethan sell this destination to his stakeholders? Admittedly, the writer made it easy for him to click on the destination's Web site, so Ethan will be prepared with facts and figures and photos for his executive meeting. Even if he does that, though, what will he say to get his counterparts excited about selecting this particular destination, especially when so many others offer the same product?

Help your prospect buy! Your sales message can prepare your buyer by clearly connecting the dots between the features and benefits that you offer and the business motivation for the product, in this case, a sales meeting.

Why do organizations hold sales meetings? The most basic goals of most sales meetings are to rally the troops and to provide product or customer education. More than that, though, the reason the majority of companies spend money on bringing their sales folks together is to give them the tools and the motivation to increase profits—to get out there and sell more. Knowing this, it's simple to give the e-mail to Ethan a much stronger selling message:

```
Hi Ethan,

Brian Matthew suggested I contact you. He told
me that you're looking for a creative, exclusive,
affordable meeting experience for your sales
leaders. I'll call you Friday to talk about how you
can feel confident that their experience at ABC will
create momentum for another successful year
of selling.
```

What's different? In the second example, the message goes beyond creating wow and sun and sand to business strategy: select us, and "you can feel confident that their experience at ABC will create momentum for another successful year of selling."

◆◆◆

By applying the language of their business to your e-mails, you provide the support your buyers need if they are to sell their "customers" on what you're selling to them.

Suppose you're talking to the owner of Kool Party Rentals, who happens to be my cousin, Jack Weiner. Kool's furnishings and accessories can be arranged in multiple patterns to provide uncommon and clever seating and dining combinations. They provide lighted furniture, leather sofas, clear acrylic tables, and all sorts of other, yes, very cool stuff. It's hard to explain, and that is exactly the point. How do I, as the buyer, persuade my executive team that I'm making a smart fiscal decision by choosing this high-end furniture as an upgrade for our meeting? After all, there are less expensive options.

The challenge is compounded because Kool's sales catalogue, with its photos of dramatic and gorgeous designs, shows only the designs and not the outcomes. There are many reasons to rent the upscale options that Kool offers, and the easier Jack can make it for the people he and his salespeople speak to to sell the business outcomes of his Kool rentals, the easier it will be for him to convert leads into solid business.

Here are just two business reasons that might resonate for a decision maker and the decision maker's boss, too:

- What is the value of having your team walk into a room that creates energy and provides a great buzz? If the event is intended to energize the team, if the venue doesn't look fun, welcoming, and exciting, the meeting won't be successful. Fun, funky, different furniture creates the ambiance and environment to get the team excited and accomplish the event goal.
- If the event is intended to thank the group for its efforts, isn't part of the event ROI (return on investment) making the event so much fun that the group works hard so that it can be treated to another party? What is the value of having attendees rave about

and remember the event? Achieving the event's goals is the ROI on the furniture.

The more you apply the language of business, the easier it is to build business (and be cool, too).

ALIGN YOUR MESSAGE WITH YOUR CUSTOMER'S NEEDS

As mentioned earlier, it's easiest to influence with beneficial outcomes. We're elevating the stakes now to ensure that those outcomes reflect your customer's initiatives.

Remember the list of customer benefits from Chapter 5? In that section, we focused only on creating brief, aspirational, powerful reader benefits. Here is part of that list. Consider how each of these outcomes will specifically align with your prospect's organizational objectives:

- **Save time.** Improved efficiency helps the organization accomplish more and produce more in less time, enabling profits.
- **Save money.** Reduced costs may help the organization flourish in a tough economy and enable it to retain and reward employees.
- **Experience less stress.** Will a harmonious work environment influence the generation of new ideas and innovative breakthroughs? Will new ideas lead to higher profit margins? Will a pleasant work environment limit hostile behavior?
- **Have fun.** Will a culture of fun drive collaboration? Will a relaxed atmosphere inspire creativity? Will employee recruiting and retention be easier because the workplace is fun?

The more you understand what features of your product or service your prospect finds important, the more your message will resonate for her. Write your e-mail so that you are the spark of inspiration that your customer needs in order to influence others.

◆◆◆

Nothing replaces knowing your buyers' real needs.

WHO KNEW SALES WRITING MEANT ALL THIS?

If you're feeling a bit overwhelmed thinking of all the aspects of sales strategy that need to be incorporated when you're writing, take heart! It's not necessary to apply each concept in every e-mail. Rather, it's important that you have a clear strategy that is based on your customers' best interests. Write from their perspective and you make it easy for them to give you the result you want.

CHAPTER 14

♦♦♦

HOW NOT TO BE YOUR OWN WORST ENEMY

It is sometimes more productive to simply say "blah" rather than "blah, blah, blah."

—DONALD E. WETMORE, PH.D.

E-mail usage, despite pundits who might suggest otherwise, continues to grow. One result of this is that we are falling further behind in keeping up with our inbox. The number of new or unread messages, according to research conducted in 2010 by Jakob Nielson, Ph.D., is 300 percent higher than it was in 2006. As we and our clients attempt to achieve a zero inbox (no pending e-mail), we hastily determine what we can safely delete. Unsolicited sales messages stand no chance of being read unless they are relevant, meaningful, and appear as eye candy to the recipient. Even follow-up e-mails, a subject that we'll get to in later chapters, must be written in a manner that encourages the reader to read them, not speed-read them.

KEEP YOUR READER'S EYES MOVING

According to speed-reading research conducted a few years ago, 67 percent of adult Americans read in what the researchers called a "Z" pattern. Our eyes take in the words in a pattern resembling the letter Z. We are in such a hurry to finish reading the message that we don't even bother to read to the end of a line—forget reading to the end of a sentence! We read clumps of words rather than sentences.

With e-mail, we often scroll as we read (much like coming to a "rolling stop" at a stop sign). We keep the "page" moving as we attempt to figure out the point of this message and move on to the next one. Sometimes we even keep our eyes in one spot as we scroll, hoping that key words will come to us, popping into our view.

One reason we don't pay attention while we read is that we don't need all the information that is coming our way, and we are content with simply taking in a snapshot preview. Another reason for our lack of attention to what others write (and, conversely, their lack of attention to what we write to them) is that we (and they) are just swamped with stuff to do. We're way past information overload; we're overwhelmed and exhausted, and we feel that we can accomplish everything (or at least more) only if we do (at least) two things at once.

Psychologist David Baldwin calls this "The Doing Two or Three Things at a Time Syndrome." He says that once we're comfortable multitasking, we actually feel uncomfortable when we're doing only one thing at a time. (I could be the poster child for this syndrome!) Many of us are so accustomed to juggling two things at once that we don't even realize we're doing it. We read our e-mail while we talk on the phone (and throw the ball to the dog). We read the proposal (which someone else labored over) while we eat lunch and listen to our counterparts at the next lunch table. Because we know that others are just as overwhelmed and we can't control what other people do (only what we do), we need to write in a manner that encourages buyers to focus their attention on our message.

Make it as easy as possible for customers to grasp your points by drawing their eye down the screen. List points, rather than present them in pure narrative form, to enable your reader to scroll down the message and still see your key issues.

When you choose to write in narrative form, break up the monotonous type pattern with headings and subheadings. Divide ideas with these headings and subheadings to enable the prospect to skim your message using that comfortable and efficient Z pattern. Headings and subheadings also help readers save time by acting as guideposts; they can scroll quickly until a heading that is relevant pops up, and then they can slow their scrolling and actually read the part that is significant. Like thumbing through a magazine in an airport gift shop to decide whether to purchase it, your reader can scroll to a point of interest without wasting valuable time.

MAKE IT APPEALING

Tony Hsieh, CEO of Zappos, in his book *Delivering Happiness*, quotes one of his favorite tweets: "A great company is more likely to die of indigestion from too much opportunity than starvation from too little. Packard's Law." This applies to e-mail writing, too. Make your e-mails eye candy—sweet to look at and easy to digest—to encourage your prospects to want to read them. Keep your sentences and paragraphs short. Use simple, clear, precise words. Make them look like they won't be a hassle or time-consuming to read, and your recipients will be more likely to read them.

In e-mail, depend less on graphic tools like bolding, colors, or funky font styles to make your point and more on clear word choices and the relevance of your information.

Here are three additional tips:

- Underlining should be used only to indicate a hyperlink.
- If you choose to bold words (and this should not be a common practice because so many people consider it shouting), be certain that the words you highlight with bold are important to the reader. Don't put into bold things that are simply procedural or helpful to you and your selling efforts.

In the examples that follow, notice *who* the bolded words talk about.

Choose this: **To ensure that you receive your widgets** by your requested date, please complete the attached form and e-mail it by September 9.

Not this: To ensure that you receive your widgets by your requested date, **please complete the attached form and e-mail it by September 9.**

Choose this: Please sign and return your agreement by Friday to confirm your menu choices. (No bold!)

Not this: Please **sign and return your agreement by Friday** to confirm your menu choices.

You may *think* you're helping your reader by highlighting the due date or a procedural step, but by highlighting the benefit to him of following the procedure, you'll create impetus for him to do it. If it doesn't benefit the reader, don't highlight it. Also, when a due date is looming, it's smart to put that type of information in the subject line and again, quietly, in the e-mail: (Subject: Action Request: Banquet Event Order deadline—12/19).

- Double space between paragraphs. The white space lets your recipient breathe between ideas. It also makes your message look less daunting.

LENGTH MATTERS

The famous philosopher Voltaire said, "The secret of being a bore is to tell everything." The last thing your customers want today is TMI (too much information), and one of the first things they notice is the length of your e-mail. Nothing spells *do not read* as much as a long, dense e-mail sales message.

Refrain from telling your reader more than he wants to know.

Some people are afraid that if they don't mention every great product or service they offer, they may miss an opportunity. (What if I don't tell them that it glows in the dark and that turns out to be exactly what really matters to them?) Yes, you may not get their business. But if 99.9 percent of your prospects don't care if their toothbrush glows in the dark, and you continue to sell this feature in your prospecting message, you're wasting time—theirs and yours!

I recently worked with a financial planner whose primary market in 2009 was affluent baby boomers. His company had just launched a creative and very smart college savings plan. The plan, designed for young families without much money, was a very exciting opportunity, but it made little sense for affluent baby boomers, whose kids were out of college (and living in the guest room). The offer could appeal to them for their grandchildren, but it was aimed at people with minimal wealth (please ignore the seeming oxymoron), not the income brackets that most of his clients had reached. He had a great product for a different buyer. Don't waste the tiny amount of time prospects may give you with secondary stuff. Be as brief as possible without being blunt, especially when you are trying to make a first impression. Strive for conciseness, and be respectful of their time.

Here are some tips to ensure crisp, clear, concise, courteous writing:

- Use short sentences and short paragraphs. Your e-mail isn't the great American novel. Its purpose is to engage the buyer, communicate a message, and persuade her to take an action. The easier it is for her to grasp your point, do it, and move on, the happier you both will be.
- Avoid words like "who was." These typically create long clauses:
  Wordy: The person who was copying the e-mails to everyone in the office should have known better.
  Better: The person copying e-mails to everyone in the office should have known better.
- Reduce phrases.
  Wordy: The speaker at the end of the meeting was the most boring.

Better: The last speaker was the most boring.
- Remove the word *that* if the sentence makes sense without it.
  Wordy: The e-mail that I wrote was forwarded to the customer.
  Better: The e-mail I wrote was forwarded to the customer.
- Avoid empty sentence starts.
  Wordy: There are three more days before the meeting.
  Better: The meeting is in three days.

The easiest way to make your e-mail look like eye candy for your reader is to practice the strategies we've been discussing since the early chapters of this book. Stay on message by planning your strategy before writing and including only information that is relevant to the reader. When you know what you want to say, you can get there without a detour.

◆◆◆

GET RESULTS, NOT RIDICULE

*Good Manners: The noise you don't make when
you're eating soup.*

—BENNETT CERF

If you walked into the grocery store wearing clothing on only the top half of your body and just, ahem, "basics" on the bottom, two things would probably happen: you'd call attention to yourself (and not in a good way), and you'd be thrown out of the store without the milk you went there for. E-mailing without attending to the guidelines that others have come to expect gets the same poor results: you become a distraction to your own message, and you don't get the result you want.

These suggestions will help your readers—customers, clients, prospects, colleagues, managers, staff, executives, associates, and more— like you better. You may even want to post these guidelines for your colleagues so that you each like one another more.

1. **Stop the high-priority flag thing**. It annoys customers and everyone else. Your e-mail about your extended discount is not my high priority. The only exception to the no high-priority flag is when your reader has indicated that your message is urgent to her. If it's a priority to her, flag it.

2. **Say "hello."** Start with a friendly, civil greeting. This is particularly important in the first e-mail you send to a recipient each day. As the day goes on and the e-mails fly between you, dropping the greeting makes perfect sense (so does picking up the phone). Just as you wouldn't simply grunt like a caveperson when you walk into the office each morning, don't ignore this simple courtesy. Start with "Hello," "Hi," or "Good morning." Be civil!

3. **Use the reader's name.** "Hi Matthew"; "Good morning Kory"; "Dear Mrs. Jones." This is an easy way to personalize, grab the reader's attention, and show warmth. If your company culture is formal or conservative, the demographic you sell to is older, or you communicate internationally, you might consider using your reader's surname instead of her first name. Always choose the formal salutation "Dear" when you are use the prospect's last name. Also, remember to use the honorific title for a doctor, a religious or political leader, and those serving in the military. Showing them the respect they've earned is more than smart business—it's the polite thing to do.

4. **Fill in the subject line.** Consider it a window to the soul of your e-mail.

5. **Use one-subject e-mails.** When you do this, your subject line can accurately reflect what the e-mail is about. If you incorporate more than one subject into the e-mail, list all the subjects in the subject line and use subheadings to distinguish your subjects within your message.

   Example: "Subject: Slide deck, conference call confirmation and logistics question"

6. **Change the subject line to match the message.** I once did a test with a client and didn't change the subject line to see if he would. After four months, I could no longer stand using "Happy Thanksgiving" and gave in. When the subject changes, so should the heading. Your e-mails are easier to file, forward, and find when the subject line accurately reflects the current message.

7. **Explain your attachment.** Even if you just say something simple such as "Here's the info I promised you" or "Hope this helps clarify yesterday's discussion," you'll make a much friendlier impression on your recipient.

8. **Don't use BCC to be sneaky.** If you want to copy someone on a message and you don't want the recipient to know you're doing it, don't do it the slimy way (and the way that can be easily discovered). Cut and paste your message and e-mail it to the other person with a note: "Just wanted you to see what I sent to Scott."

9. **Use BCC to protect the confidentiality of addresses and to avoid a major blob of e-mail addresses at the start of your e-mail.** (Notice that BCC is a good idea when it isn't being used for nefarious purposes.)

10. **Clean your message.** Eliminate all but the last message or two from your e-mail thread. One client sent me a writing example that when I printed it out to show to him had a thread at least 16 feet long! Even worse, as I was taping the pages together to create a thread scroll to make my point, I read the back messages. There was proprietary information that had been sent inadvertently to a customer.

11. **"S.O.R.T.A." Stamp Out Reply To All.** Be thoughtful about whom you're sending your response to. Just because 18 people were copied on the original, do all 18 need to know your response? Really?

12. **Eliminate return receipt requests.** The implication of these requests is neither trusting nor pleasant. If you think your reader will lie to you about receiving your message, you have a problem that's beyond the scope of this book! If you really need to know if he's received your e-mail, call him, ask him to confirm receipt, or at a minimum be up front about the return receipt request. You might say: "As soon as I receive confirmation from you, I'll place a hold on the space," or, "Because so many messages seem to go straight to the spam folder, I'd be grateful if you would confirm that this e-mail went where it was intended—to

you!" or, "I've attached a return receipt request so we'll both have documentation." Or, use a version of the trick I used when my son was in college to motivate him to respond to me. I'd write, "Also, I notice you didn't cash the check I mailed you as a surprise. Did you receive it?" You just can't imagine how quickly I'd get a response back.

13. **If you attach something, mention it.** Don't expect the prospect to read your mind and scroll to the bottom of the message to see if, maybe, you attached something. Also, position your attachment so that it shows just before your signature line, instead of after it.

14. **Don't be lazy.** It is so tempting to find an old e-mail, hit Reply, and start writing about something that had nothing to do with the original message. Instead of using old e-mails to communicate, start fresh.

15. **Use a closing.** You need to use a closing, but it shouldn't be Ciao (unless you're in Italy) or Cheers! (unless you're in the United Kingdom) or in any language you don't speak. Closings are personal and choices exist, but they don't include pretense. Depending on your organizational brand, here are some choices to consider:

    • All the best.
    • Wishing you all the best.
    • Warm regards.
    • Warmest regards.
    • Thank you. (Use this as a close only *if* you have something to thank the person about, more than that she just read your message.)

      Avoid "Take care" and "Best of luck." The reader may think you know something that she doesn't.

      Using "Best" and "Regards" can be considered too abrupt. "Best regards" or "Warm regards" is better.

      "Sincerely," Cordially," and "Respectfully" can be used when the message is formal or you're writing internationally. These closings are best reserved for letterhead stationery and not used for e-mail.

"Talk soon" can be used once a relationship is established, but "Later" is a bit too informal (and I always want to add "alligator" to "Later"—sad, but true).

Use the same closing that the other person uses in his e-mail to you.

16. **Save the world on your own time.** Your personal philosophy of life is just that, yours, and it should not be included in your signature line. Not only do you run the risk of offending a prospect, but you can also sound pompous and arrogant. A senior consultant added this quote to every e-mail: "The pessimist complains about the wind. The optimist expects it to change. The leader adjusts the sail. John C. Maxwell." I never figured out if he thought that he modeled that behavior or thought that I should.

17. **Use the "To" line for the person you expect to respond to your message.** If you need to copy others, with no expectation of a response, put them on the CC line.

18. **Include the original message you're responding to unless it says something that should not have been put in writing.** If it does, start a fresh e-mail and cut and paste the parts that can be repeated.

19. **Respond within the list.** When you receive a list of questions, respond directly after each question. For courtesy's sake, you might write: "For your convenience, my answers follow." If you choose to answer in CAPS (and you can; this is an exception to the rule that CAPS mean shouting), mention it immediately ("My answers follow in CAPS to make them easy to see"). You can also put angle brackets—<< these are angle brackets>>—around your responses or use colors. Whatever you choose to do to separate your answers from the questions, explain it before you do it. Also, answer kindly. Remember that the point of the e-mail isn't just to provide information but to provide confidence in your answers.

20. **If you expect a response, clue in the other person!** Just because you send an e-mail doesn't mean that the other person is obli-

gated to respond. Explain to your reader: "I'll follow up as you suggest," or, "I'll look forward to receiving your response to . . . ," or, "As soon I receive your confirmation, I'll. . . ."

21. **Thank her only once.** Everyone is entitled to send a thank you. But a thank you for a thank you is a time waster. It's not a holiday gift exchange, so don't worry about giving her back something equal. I thank you. You thank me. Stop. (If you really feel a need to send a more significant thank you, use nice stationery and handwrite your message.)

22. **Don't overpunctuate.** Multiple !!!!! may make folks think you forgot to take your meds today. Unless someone just got married, had a baby, or landed a new contract, use only one exclamation point. Even worse than multiple !!!!, however, is multiple ?????. What is it you're really saying with all those question marks?

    Another overused punctuation device is ellipsis points. As discussed, avoid using them in a subject line, and use them only infrequently in the body of the e-mail. I have a friend who uses so many . . . in her e-mails that I sometimes think she is sending an SOS message. You can use the dot, dot, dot to indicate missing words or a thought break, but one . . . often leads to another . . . and to. . . . Enough said. Except for this: creating an ellipsis with commas (,,,) is never acceptable.

23. **If you forward a message to a group of people, send it to yourself and add the other addresses in the BCC line.**

24. **If you ask someone to phone you, provide your phone number directly after your request.** Even if it's in your signature line, be nice to your reader. Instead of making him scroll to the location where it was convenient for you to include it, write it where he can stop (tap) and call back. This is also true for fax numbers. When you want your recipient to fax, include the fax number with your request.

25. **Respond so that she knows.** If you can't respond in full immediately, acknowledge receiving her e-mail and say when you can. To ignore the message entirely is bad form. Here is a message I wrote to an associate yesterday: "Thanks for your call and fol-

low-up e-mail. I'm in Australia and can get back to you on this on Feb. 9. If this isn't okay, please let me know and I'll try to make it happen sooner."

If a customer requests a full-blown proposal by noon, acknowledge the request and tell her when you'll have it for her. You also may need to explain why it will take longer and offer to provide a partial proposal within her time frame.

If a counterpart sends you a link to a YouTube video that she thinks is hysterical and you're knee deep in whatever, you can still take the time to respond: "Thanks for thinking of me. Swamped now, but will definitely watch this—though it may be next month!"

If someone sends you mail that you consider junk, stop him from wasting your time while acknowledging his positive intent. You might write (or say over the phone):

```
Hi Name,

I appreciate the motivational messages you send
each Monday, but without meaning to be offensive,
I'd appreciate it if you'd take me off your
distribution list. I'm swamped, and as much as
I can use encouragement, I also need to empty my
inbox, do my work, see my family, and get some
sleep! Please be sure to take me off the list
today, and thanks for thinking of me.
```

◆◆◆

Always represent yourself as the professional you are.

26. **Don't tell others when they must get back to you unless you also provide them with a pleasant reason for doing so.**
    Don't say: Respond by Friday.
    Say: Your response by Friday guarantees room availability.

Don't say: Your credit application is due Monday.

Say: To ensure that your credit application is processed quickly, please complete the application by Monday.

27. **Use a font that people can read.** Size and style matter.

28. **Don't end by asking, "What do you think?"** Simplify your reader's response and encourage her to give you the result you want by offering your opinion and asking for her approval:

    Don't say: What do you think about these ideas?

    Don't say: Your reply, please.

    Don't say: Please respond.

    Say: Please let me know which direction you prefer, and with your approval, I'll move forward.

    Say: Please let me know if you'd like me to move forward with this.

29. **Depend on words, not emoticons.** The saying "A picture is worth a thousand words" is true. Sometimes, one ;-) can say it all. Like excess exclamation points or question marks, however, if you use too many of them, your reader may think you got stuck in junior high (or worse, MySpace!). Prefer robust, vigorous words over emoticons to convey your message.

30. **Avoid sending inadvertent messages.** I travel all the time, and no one ever knows what time zone or country I'm in (sometimes even I don't!). Because of this, I can get away with writing to clients at all hours, although I still occasionally receive a response to a late-night e-mail that starts with, "What were you doing awake at 3 a.m.?" The inadvertent messages sent by the hour you e-mail might be: you're overwhelmed and can't take good care of the client, the client isn't important enough for you to take care of her during regular hours, or she's an afterthought. If you're writing to the members of your own team at all hours, they may think that you expect them to keep the same crazy hours, or to check their e-mail when they get up to use the toilet in the night! Save messages in your draft box to send during standard working hours.

31. **Don't sip and send.** Regardless of what time you're writing, don't e-mail a client after a couple of cocktails. What sounds oh-

so-clever often isn't when it's viewed in the light of the sobering morning sun.

32. **Don't use e-mail to gossip.** Third-person criticism has an amazing way of being forwarded to the very person who is being criticized. June Kronholtz said, "Diamonds are forever. E-mail comes close." E-mail that is critical of people is almost guaranteed to live in perpetuity. If you have something to say, pick up the phone.

Take the time to be mannerly. It can't hurt, and it certainly may help your reputation and your sales efforts.

❖❖❖

CHAPTER 16

E-MAIL ON A SMARTPHONE: USE THIS, NOT THAT

While the text and format of the message hasn't changed much, how we use email as a communications tool has completely morphed.

—MITCH JOEL

Like any best friend relationship, my relationship with my iPhone is conflicted. I love her, and she is always there for me, but as much as she insists that she helps me save time and do things more smartly (it's even part of her nickname!), she also takes up a lot of my time and sometimes makes me look dumb. I'm always on the go with her, and it's true that when I'm in a rush, I sometimes get lazy about adhering to standard business communication practices and have, quite frankly, developed poor habits when I'm around her.

Okay. I'll stop now, but I bet this whine sounds familiar.

To avoid wasting time and looking less than brilliant when you use your smartphone as you do when you keyboard to communicate with your customers (external and internal), apply these tips:

1. **Identify repetitive requests that you receive and create awe-inspiring templates to use.** Create e-mail signature file templates, or "canned responses" on Gmail, for the common requests so that you can respond quickly and professionally from your smartphone.

   Most salespeople, for instance, receive frequent e-leads but don't have the time or the appropriate information to respond immediately in a thoughtful and thorough manner. By creating a template acknowledging the request and letting the prospect know when to expect the requested information, you can easily use your smartphone to send e-mails that extend your professional business image. (Create the templates on your laptop and you can use them from there, too.)

   A template, kept as an e-mail signature file, might say:

```
Hi _____,


You've come to the right place! You and your
associates will be E-mail Ninjas after they
complete a customized Power Sales Writing workshop.

You can count on receiving the requested
information by DATE, and I'll follow up with you
on DATE. If you'd like the information more quickly,
please let me know so I can meet your deadline.

I'm eager to help your team convert more leads
into solid business!

All the best.

Standard signature line stuff
```

   Think about all the common e-mail requests you receive. Develop meaningful message templates that require you to insert minimal personalization (or none) to use your smartphone efficiently and effectively.

2. **In general, reply only to the person who is sending the e-mail, not to everyone on the CC list.** There are few things more aggravating than being the recipient of 12 people's RSVPs: "I'll be there." "I'll be there." "Should be able to make it." "I'll be there, but I may be late." "Will be there." "I'll be there." "Can't go, will be in London." "I'll be there." "Count me in." "Yes." "I'll be there, too." "Me too."

   Certainly there are some situations when it's best to hit Reply To All, but those usually don't include meeting invitations. The last thing you want is to start a daisy chain of e-mail responses from your phone.

3. **Reread your message for those notorious autopopulate spelling errors.** Even folks who studiously check the e-mails they write on their laptops ignore this when they're using their smartphones.

4. **Use traditional business format.** Here is how it looks:
   Greeting
   Message
   Close
   Signature line
   Contact information

5. **Text only with the recipient's approval.** Even if he agrees, don't text a client before 7 a.m. or after 9 p.m. unless he asks you to. It's likely that he uses his phone as his alarm clock too, and the little beep indicating an incoming text message is more than a bit unwelcome before or after standard business hours. Also, keep in mind that your text messages can be kept and forwarded. The same rules that apply to smart business writing also apply to smart business texting.

6. **Don't abbreviate.** If you wouldn't abbreviate words in an e-mail you'd send to your customer from your laptop (and you shouldn't), don't abbreviate just because you're e-mailing from a smartphone or texting.

7. **Consider treating mail that you send from your smartphone no differently from mail that you write from your laptop or**

computer. As @AdamSchomaker responded to my tweet asking how e-mail has evolved with the use of smartphones: "I really do nothing different in e-mail. My signatures match, bodies are the same. It's important for my brand to not look different."

Smart sales professionals take advantage of every possible tool to give themselves a selling edge. They know that when everyone is using the written word, if they are to stand out, their words need to be more respectful, more focused, and more engaging.

Whether you communicate by text or by telephone, e-mail, or standard postal message, your prospect is looking for clues to your reliability, credibility, and likability. Excellent e-mail messages are a great place to show off your stuff.

◆◆◆

Get your ideas across, smartly.

PART FIVE

◆◆◆

KEEPING CUSTOMERS HAPPY

Question: Isn't it really "customer helping" rather than "customer service"? And wouldn't you deliver better service if you thought of it that way?

—JEFFREY GITOMER

Customers can be unhappy for all sorts of reasons. You don't have what they want; you have what they want, but it's too expensive, too inexpensive, or the wrong size, color, design, dates, or delivery; you did something they didn't expect; you didn't do something they did expect; you ignored them; you pestered them; you breathed funny, smelled bad, or were not bad or fun enough.

Sometimes we're the ones who are displeased. We don't get the raise we think we deserve; we don't get the meeting with the customer's boss that was promised; we don't get the pricing we want to offer from our revenue manager.

It's difficult to write to customers who are distressed, and its even more challenging to write when we are distressed. This section helps you communicate your message in a more powerful and profitable manner, even when you're under pressure and the situation is difficult. By applying these ideas to your e-mail messaging, you'll communicate more persuasively, whether you're trying to convince your sales manager to give you back your old territory, persuade a reluctant customer to reorder before the end of the month (so that you meet your quota), or influence a disgusted client who is fed up with your service, your prices, and (from his e-mail, it sounds like) even your lineage to give you one more chance.

Use these ideas to enhance your potential and your sales success.

CHAPTER 17

◆ ◆ ◆

WRITE "BAD NEWS" MESSAGES—AND KEEP CUSTOMERS HAPPY

Great leaders are always great simplifiers who can cut through argument, debate and doubt to offer a solution everyone can understand.

—COLIN POWELL, FORMER U.S. SECRETARY OF STATE

Hostile readers. What an unsavory way to describe those people whom you've disappointed, frustrated, aggravated, and, in general, annoyed (through real or imaginary actions) to such a degree that when they receive an e-mail from you, they read it with a chip on their shoulder and their finger hovering over the Delete button.

Hostile readers can be those customers to whom you promised absolute on-time delivery of their printing job, but you experienced a major press breakdown, so they had to leave for the trade show without their printing—that is, with no collateral.

Hostile readers can be those clients who agreed to an attrition clause when they (and you) expected no problem with attrition. Because of world events, they had a huge drop-off in their numbers; you need them to live up to the agreement they made with you, and they think you're being unreasonable.

Hostile readers can be those loyal customers who were shocked—shocked, I say!—at your new pricing structure, your change in packaging, or your new, highly impersonal, automated ordering system.

In general, hostile readers are those people who have been either disappointed by something you've done or disappointed because you haven't done something.

The biggest challenge a writer has is to make certain that her words are understood the way she intended them to be understood.

Let's imagine that you have a customer request for something that doesn't fit within your sales strategy. For instance, maybe the entire Hershkowitz clan would like to meet in your hotel for a reunion over a prime selling weekend. It doesn't take a revenue expert to figure out that reunion business over Super Bowl weekend isn't going to yield the greatest profit potential. The Hershkowitz family is aware that its reunion business may not be highly coveted, which is exactly why a family member contacted you immediately after the Super Bowl location was announced.

The family is hopeful, and you're about to dash its hopes. Depending on how you respond to the request, however, you have the opportunity to maintain the family's loyalty to your hotel, even though you cannot accept the business, or not maintain it.

How will you respond to this e-mail request? What will you write to avoid holding space you are confident you'll sell at a much higher rate and still keep the Hershkowitz family happy?

The first step, naturally, is to consider both your writing and your sales strategy by asking the five planning questions:

1. *Why?* To excite the family about a fun reunion on an alternative date or at a different hotel.
2. *What?* Your family can have the best time ever at DEF Hotel (located in another city, and available for your preferred dates) or at your preferred hotel, ABC (four or eight months after the requested date).
3. *Accomplish?* Maintain goodwill and move the family to another date, space, or time.
4. *Next step?* Hershkowitz e-mails me back to tell me her preference.
5. *Delighter?* Your family event will be fun, memorable, and very special at DEF.

Because your goal is to avoid losing the business by selling her on another possibility, you might write:

Hi Ms. Hershkowitz,

Thank you for considering the ABC Hotel for your family reunion. It is a perfect hotel for all age groups because it's located near parks and excellent hiking trails.

Another excellent option is the DEF Hotel. It, too, is situated among some of the best nature paths and family-friendly venues anywhere. Each sleeping room has a small kitchen and refrigerator, something many groups find preferable to a standard hotel room. And the best part is that it has space available over the February dates of your planned reunion!

If you prefer to get together at ABC, available dates are June 2-4 and November 4-6. Because of the amount of space required, these are the only options at this time.

```
Please let me know if you'd like me to hold the space
at DEF. Your family will have fun and make lots of
special new memories!
```

What if you had written:

```
Hi,

The dates you requested are not available. Thank you
for considering the ABC Hotel.
```

Short? Yes. Sweet? No. Don't sell yourself short by rejecting your prospects! In almost every sales situation, there is an option that can help the prospect. Offer it. It may not be the ideal solution, but it is a solution. In the reunion case, if the family's desire is to meet in your city because it was midway between where the various members lived, changing the date may be fine. Maybe your brand is important to them (frequent stay points or other perks) and they are happy to switch dates, or maybe they would prefer to stay in another city because the preferred dates are the *only* dates the family members can all get together. Offer options to keep customers happy.

By planning your strategy (offering an alternative solution), you can neutralize a negative situation and possibly create an option that leads to delighted customers and booked business. Will your customer always be thrilled with your alternative solution? Maybe not. You will, however, maintain loyalty and the possibility of additional sales opportunities.

What if you can't offer an alternative? What if the E-mail Ninja Kits are on back order for 13 months and the alternative solution is sending her to a competitor offering the Almost E-mail Ninja Kits for double the price? Tell her! This may be a solution that satisfies her at least temporarily or she may be willing to wait. You can look like a hero for making an alternative solution available and have the opportunity to follow up, creating an authentic relationship.

SET THE TONE

Beginning an e-mail by saying thank you is not the most powerful way to start. There are many other ways to start that are less common and more meaningful to your recipient. When responding with "bad news," however, you sometimes don't have many choices. With a goal of starting the message in an authentic, pleasant, and friendly manner, saying thank you can be your best option. When you are writing to readers who might be upset by the news you're about to give them, saying thank you can neutralize the situation. "Thank you for asking for clarification" or "Thank you for taking the time to write" helps the reader feel safe and smart.

Another opportunity to begin your e-mail with a thank you comes when you're responding to a complaint. "Thank you for giving me the opportunity to explain this situation" is a genuine, honest sentiment. Your customer has given you the opportunity to explain the situation so that you can educate him, satisfy him, and win him back. You are thankful, or you should be.

◆◆◆

Every interaction counts. Never stop selling your good name.

Here is another example. A loyal customer e-mails you asking for a donation for an upcoming raffle. This is the ten thousandth request your company has received this year and the third from this customer's organization. Just last week, management sent a companywide e-mail that essentially said, "No more freebies."

Whether you agree with management's perspective or not, you need to turn down the customer and still maintain his loyalty. Here is an e-mail I recently read that attempted to do just that:

```
Brady,

I would so love to donate X to your organization's
raffle, but the big boss has sent out a mandate: no
```

```
more freebies! I even spoke to her personally to see
if I could get an exception for you because you're
such a great customer. No deal. She isn't buying.

Sorry, friend. Wish I had better news.
```

I am hopeful that you're aghast at this message. To blame her refusal on company policy (in any form), to make the customer's request seem cheesy (a freebie), and then to try to make herself into a hero by throwing her boss under the bus . . . I'm speechless.

High-achieving sales reps never ever shift blame. Not to the big boss, company policy, or their kid's soccer game. Instead, they create solutions and options to please the customer. This requires integrity, strategy, and planning.

Here are the writing and sales goals as I see them:

1. *Why?* To help Brady explain to his stakeholders why we are loyal partners and why they should continue their relationship with us regardless of this donation.
2. *What?* You'll be proud to know that we've supported A, B, and C; I'm happy to volunteer for your event.
3. *Accomplish?* Maintain Brady's loyalty, friendship, and revenue.
4. *Next step?* Brady lets me know if I can volunteer.
5. *Delighter?* You can be proud to work with a company that's rooted in community values.

Take a few minutes to write an e-mail to Brady that will achieve your writing goals.

Here is the sales message I might write:

```
Hi Brady,

Thank you for thinking of ABC to help you create
excitement for your raffle. I would love to volunteer
to help make your raffle a huge success. If I can help
you sell tickets, please let me know.
```

```
The XYZ Company contributes more than $$$$$ each
year to important causes like yours, and decisions
are made through corporate headquarters. I've
included the application for you so that the XYZ
cause can be considered for next year. I would love
to see this added to those we can affect because of
the good work you do.

Brady, if I can personally help you, please let me
know. It would be my pleasure to donate my time to
this important cause.
```

Of course, if Brady isn't as good a friend as the original e-mail implied, or if the cause isn't one that you care to support, you'll need to look for a different solution. Maybe the only option you can offer is the donation application. The point is to write to help the other person maintain face. You've given Brady the information he needs to understand and easily report to his management team why you turned him down. Though a rejection, Brady won't feel alienated, and just the opposite might happen. You've educated him about what good corporate citizens you are, and this may be a great selling point when your contract comes up for renewal next month.

Here is one more: imagine that you've been late to work for four days in a row. (For some of you, this isn't difficult to envision.) You get an e-mail from your manager, and all it says is:

```
You've been late to work four times this week. This
is not acceptable behavior.
```

What is your reaction? I don't know how sweet you are, but I'd be tempted to e-mail back, pounding my keys: "You want acceptable behavior? I'll show you acceptable behavior. First, pay me more. I'll buy a helicopter, avoid all the traffic, and be at this lousy job on time, your majesty. But I digress because I always meet my quota, don't I? Why don't you ever talk to Jacob? He is here on time every day, but he couldn't sell water in a desert in the summer. And speaking of the desert, I'm going to Arizona on vacation next week. I won't just be late. I won't even be here."

When someone attacks or offends us, our bodies immediately respond to the threat of danger. Our initial, primitive response is to either fight the attacker or flee from the abuse. (This is that "fight or flight" phenomenon we learned about in Psych 101.) Verbal and written attacks have the same initial effect on our system as the threat of a physical attack.

Powerful writers understand that it's not necessarily what we say but how we say it that can persuade our prospect, spouse, friend, colleague, or boss in one direction or another. The way in which those words are presented has a huge effect on their acceptability and the response they elicit.

USE AN AUTHENTIC AND SOLUTION-ORIENTED BUFFER

```
Dear Mom and Dad,

I'm sending you this e-mail from a friend's computer
because my computer was destroyed in the fire in
my apartment. Just the other day, I got out of the
hospital and moved in with Buster, my boyfriend. Your
new grandbaby is due next fall.

Your loving daughter, Tiffany

P.S. None of the above is true. I did, however, make
a D in Chemistry and an F in Chinese, and I wanted
you to see this in its proper perspective.
```

Some people confuse the word *buffer* with the word *bull*. These people think they have to be sweet as sugar or they must somehow be manipulative if they are to get their way. They might write something like this:

```
Paul:

You did a great job with the Scottsdale project,
and I applaud you for the work you've done so far
on Nantucket. I'm glad Nancy suggested that you
join the team. It's been nice getting to know you
better. You've shown great team spirit, commitment,
and enthusiasm, and if that is needed anywhere, it's
needed on this new project. Nantucket is a huge
project and very important to the reputation of this
company. The fact is, however, that the concept
for Nantucket is entirely different from the
Scottsdale project, and you've shown no originality
whatsoever . . .
```

The writer's "bull" is obvious. This isn't selling a solution; it's manipulating one. The writer did nothing but patronize his "customer"; his response is not so different from saying to someone, "You're ugly and I need a favor." His attempt at softening the message is almost as bad as the totally opposite approach:

```
This is junk. Be more original for Nantucket.
```

Your job as a sales professional is to help the recipient of your e-mail feel safe about continuing to read your e-mail so that he feels comfortable enough with you to allow you to advance to the next step in the sale. The opening of your message should set a positive, authentic tone and establish an inviting path for the reader to follow.

Here is a truth (and I didn't have to be the sharpest knife in the drawer to come up with this): if you offend, annoy, or put off your readers or make them feel uncomfortable, incompetent, and insecure, they're likely to delete your message without reading it to its conclusion. If they don't read what you've written, you have little or no chance of getting what you want.

The writer of that last e-mail would have had better success with Paul if he had buffered the bad news, instead of trying to throw the bull:

```
Hi Paul,

Thank you for your ideas on how to move forward with
Nantucket. Your creativity was the cornerstone for
the success of the Scottsdale project, and we need
that type of originality to make Nantucket work.

The Nantucket project requires a different direction
if it is to be highly successful. Our presentation
to the client is next Monday. Your creativity will
be needed so fresh designs can be ready by Thursday,
which will give us time to meet with Everett to
discuss our strategy. Will Thursday morning or
afternoon work best for you to review your new
concepts before meeting with Everett?

Please let me know what time works for you. Let's
schedule a couple of hours to work together on the
presentation, and I'll coordinate the time with
Everett after we're both comfortable with the
creative design.
```

BE POSITIVE EVEN IF YOU FEEL LIKE SCREAMING

Some writers just can't stand the dichotomy of being positive and friendly when what they really want to say is, "&#^& you and your mama, too!"

My advice for writers who are angry or frustrated and just can't seem to get over themselves or the injustice of the situation (when you have practically worked yourself to death, doing everything possible for the client, bending over backward, pulling favors, missing family dinners, piano recitals, and soccer games) is this: don't worry about being positive!

Write the letter—on paper, not on a computer—the way you want to. Call the person every name in the book (if that is your style). Yes, swear at him, and at his mama, his dog, and his entire family tree, if that makes you feel better. Write about every single thing he could possibly have done that was stupid, mean, thoughtless, and way less than professional. List everything you've done to please him. Get all the venom and frustration out of your system and onto that paper (not screen!). Then, when you're sure it's totally out of you, when you have written it all down, shred the document. Throw part of it away in one trash can, throw another part in another trash can, and burn the remaining evidence if you won't set off the fire alarm.

This catharsis, this purging of your negativity, allows you to regain your balance and clarity and write more professionally with a positive purpose. Even the sweetest among us will have trouble keeping the bile down and the sarcasm in check when we feel we've been wronged and our feelings are hurt. Every woman (and even quite a few men) understands that talking out an issue—not necessarily solving it, just talking it out—makes it easier to understand and handle. Talk out your anger on the page. Get it out of you so that you can move on.

THE EDUCATIONAL BUFFER IS A BRIDGE

The buffer is a bridge that allows your readers to move from "What the heck can she possibly say that will mean anything to me?" to a more positive reaction like "That *is* true," or "That was nice," or some other kind thought that motivates them to keep reading instead of immediately hitting the Delete button.

Do you remember the situation from earlier in this chapter—the one where you've been late to work four days in a row? Your manager sent you this e-mail:

```
You've been late to work four times this week. This
is not acceptable behavior.
```

He could have buffered his message by writing this way:

```
Hi Daniel,

As an important part of the sales team, you're needed
in the office during core working hours (8:00 a.m.-
3:30 p.m.). For the past four days, you've come in
between 8:15 a.m. and 8:40 a.m. Please let me know if
something has happened that you cannot be here on
time. If not, please confirm that you'll be here by
8:00 a.m.
```

Isn't this buffered opening less likely to provoke a nasty comment on the part of the reader and more likely to evoke a positive response, such as, "Busted. I'll be on time from now on."

Buffers neutralize a hot situation. They aren't manipulative; they're smart.

So, let's say you received the first e-mail from your director of sales (who is clearly one crayon short of a full box). What can you do to elevate the situation and respond in a persuasive manner? First, determine your purpose for responding:

1. *Why?* To let him know he is right
2. *What?* You're right; I should have informed you of my car situation.
3. *Accomplish?* Maintain goodwill and my job.
4. *Next step?* I meet with my boss at his convenience.
5. *Delighter?* I'll work overtime, or at home, prior to arriving.

How would you buffer your message without sounding like a suck-up? It might sound something like this:

```
Hi David,

Thank you for giving me the opportunity to clarify.
You're right; I should have let you know about my
car situation and late work arrivals. I thought
I could work it out and still be in the office by
8 a.m., but I can't. Do you have a few minutes to
discuss possible solutions? I should have the car
repaired by next week, but that still may mean a few
more days of late arrivals.
```

The words "You're right" are magical when they're genuine. You remind the recipient how smart he is, which also, coincidentally, disarms him and enables him to be open to your message. The buffer should not sound like a day at the park. It should, however, prepare the reader so that he will continue to read rather than trashing the e-mail before he understands the situation.

◆◆◆

Every message, even those to hostile readers, needs to engage the recipient, sell him on your point, and invite him to buy into your idea.

Here's another situation. Earlier this year, your company instituted a policy requiring a 50 percent deposit on all orders. One longtime client has refused to make the appropriate deposit. Until last month, you delivered to her anyway. You explained to her that delivery would stop in November (13 months after the policy was instituted) unless the appropriate deposit was received. You left a voice mail for her two days before she was expecting her November delivery. You reminded her that the order had never been confirmed because no deposit had been received, and so there would be no delivery.

You're on the road, and you get a furious (make that obscene and livid) voice message from her. Without your delivery, she can't deliver to her customers, and she screams, "You will ruin me."

You are three time zones away, and it's after 9 p.m. where she is, but because you know she is likely to check her e-mail, you write to her.

How would you buffer this message? Part of the answer depends on what you hope to accomplish with your e-mail. (Always begin by knowing your purpose.)

1. *Why?* To help her get her delivery through compliance with the policy.
2. *What?* She can be assured of delivery within 24 hours, once the deposit is paid.
3. *Accomplish?* Keep her as a customer and persuade her to transfer the funds.
4. *Next step?* She confirms the deposit transfer and we schedule delivery.
5. *Delighter?* You receive lower prices because of this policy.

The e-mail could start with this educational buffer:

Hi Name,

Your customers can receive their widgets within 24 hours.

Please copy me on the requested bank transfer so I can confirm your shipment and track it for immediate delivery. (I've attached a copy of the routing form for you.)

Because of our long-term relationship, the former delivery policy was extended to you for an additional 13 months. To ensure we can maintain our industry low pricing for you and your customers, we must now require payment prior to distribution.

Please phone me anytime on my mobile (555-555-5555) and I'll plan to phone you first thing in the morning if we have not yet connected.

Buffers often accomplish their purpose (calming the reader and encouraging him to read further) in one sentence. To get the result you want, focus on soothing your reader with a sincere and truthful buffer. Remember, without the reader's buy-in, you get nothing done. By making it reasonable for your reader to continue reading and to agree with your solution, you increase your chances of maintaining a good working relationship with him and getting the result you want.

CHAPTER 18

◆◆◆

WHAT TO SAY WHEN "I'M SORRY" DOESN'T WORK

The first thing we do, let's kill all the lawyers.

—WILLIAM SHAKESPEARE, *HENRY VI, PART II*

Number 9 on the list of the American Film Industry's top 100 romantic movies of all time is *Love Story*. Rent the video if you want to know the whole story. The point that matters here is that as the original female lead (Ali McGraw) is dying, her husband (Ryan O'Neal) starts apologizing for a bunch of stuff. She stops him and (poignantly and tearfully) says, "Love means never having to say you're sorry."

Whether love means that or something different is up to you. But not saying you're sorry *is* a great business practice and one that you should certainly adhere to when you communicate in writing.

Before this entire concept makes you want to post evil thoughts about me, please understand that I recognize that most of us were raised to say three magic phrases: "please," "thank you," and "I'm sorry." With these social courtesies mastered, we were assured that life would go forward like a bowl of cherries. As children, we got out of all sorts of predicaments by using those magic phrases. We could forget to brush our teeth, lie and say we did, and if we told our mommy

"I'm sorry" (about any of it), we could still get a bedtime story read to us. We could flush our goldfish down the toilet, and if the "I'm sorry" was accompanied by tears and we were under the age of five, nothing much happened to us.

"I'm sorry" was the perfect phrase until around the age of eight. Then they changed the rules on us. We got new, more complicated requirements. We still needed to apologize, but all of a sudden, we had to accompany the apology with a different plan for the next time—what we would do better or differently instead of repeating the wrong behavior.

If we wrecked the car, saying "I'm sorry" was no longer the panacea it had once been. If we cheated on a test, "I'm sorry" didn't mean much. If we forgot to let the dog out because we stayed out with friends and he pooped all over the rug, "I'm sorry" wasn't going to save us.

Yet when we get into the world of business, we somehow think that "I'm sorry" can still work its magic for us. We revert, believing that a heartfelt apology will cover us when we've disappointed customers and not delivered for colleagues.

The apology slides off our lips and even more easily into our e-mails. How many e-mails do you see that start with "I'm sorry," sometimes with the addition of the word *so*, as in "I'm soooooooo sorry." It's true, the writer is sorry. But—drum roll, please—the apology, no matter how sincere, doesn't fix the situation. What an apology can do is help the apology giver feel better about himself and the mess that he caused; it does very little for the receiver.

If you are late with a delivery, for instance, and the customer is furious that it won't arrive until tomorrow, your apology does nothing for the customer. Rather than relying on an apology, start your message (phone first, then follow-up your phone message with an e-mail) by telling her when she can expect what wasn't provided. Focus on the solution to the quandary she is now in (because of something you've done—or not done), and then, if you feel that an apology will also help, offer it.

◆ ◆ ◆

You can always send roses, but first fix the problem. Focus on the solution before making an apology.

Service recovery, especially by e-mail, is a delicate task. When you begin by providing solutions to the problem that you caused, your customer will be more accepting of your heartfelt apology.

LAWYERS, LITIGATION, AND LIABILITY

There is another critical reason to avoid apologizing in writing: once you admit your wrongdoing and put it in writing, you run the risk of causing expensive litigation.

A tire company customer serviceperson empathized with a customer who claimed that he had lost his job because of a problem with his tire. The customer claimed that he was on his way to work when he saw a problem in his wife's tire. He didn't want her to drive on the tire, so he took her car to get the tire fixed. While he was at the tire store, a client called his company looking for him. No one could locate either him (his phone was out of charge) or the information that the client needed. Exasperated, the client canceled his account with the company. When the sales guy arrived at work after having the tire fixed, he was fired.

The salesperson, with nothing to do and plenty of time on his hands, sent an e-mail to the tire company explaining that he had been fired because of the low-quality tires the tire company sells (his reasoning, not mine). The customer service rep, on behalf of the tire company, responded, "We are sorry about the defect you found in your tire." That sentence—that apology and admission of guilt—was enough to cause the tire company to settle the claim out of court for $20,000.

I told that story while working with an international hotel group. The director of national sales practically jumped out of his seat. "We are undergoing identical litigation," he said.

A new hotel salesperson had told the meeting planner for a large association that she would hold a block of rooms for three weeks. Nothing was put in writing. She held the block for three weeks and then, when she had heard nothing and without e-mailing, released the rooms. Two months later, the planner called to book the rooms and was told that they were no longer available. The planner didn't understand. He claimed that he had been in the hospital and that a message had been left for the hotel salesperson telling her that he would call when he was recuperating. She claimed that she had never received such a message. He was furious and, over the phone, became verbally abusive to her. In an effort to avoid making the situation worse, she decided to write a letter of apology to him. She e-mailed the following apology: "I am sorry I did not hold the block of rooms for you. I should have phoned you before releasing them."

Bingo! His lawyers now had the perfect case.

I was planning to promote my speaking and training services with an exhibit booth at a trade show in Manhattan. I purchased the booth space, and when I realized how very low I was on printed brochures (who uses this stuff anymore except at trade shows?), I hired a printer in New York City to print high-quality one-page promotional brochures. The printing sales rep promised to deliver my brochures to me at the show. We were in constant contact. I was assured that the delivery of my brochures would take place at 10:00 a.m., three hours prior to the start of the show.

Ten o'clock, the appointed time, came and went. No printing. I called the company. No one could locate my order, or my sales rep. At 1:00 p.m., as the doors to the show opened, my sales rep came rushing in. He was profusely apologetic. He was so sorry, so very sorry, sooooooo sorry, but there had been a press breakdown and he was unable to get me my printing.

What did his apology do for me? Did it solve my problem? I was at an expensive trade show with no collateral to offer the attendees who stopped at my booth! Those printed promotional pieces were part of my sales strategy for the show!

What was it I wanted? I wanted brochures! I needed to know when he would get my printing to me, when I could expect black-and-white copies instead of four-color, or when he would deliver USB drives with the data on them for me to give out!

This is important: *he* may have felt better because of his mea culpa, but a solution was what *I* needed in order to feel better.

Your readers want solutions to their problems, not apologies for yours.

Some workshop attendees have pointed out that they often hear their customers say, "All I really wanted was an apology." Notice, however, when the customer says that. Usually it is only after being totally frustrated, ignored, and disrespected, and just before jumping to the competitor, that the customer says, "All I wanted was . . ." What the customer wanted was someone to listen, to care, and to show concern and respect. That is exactly what we do when we focus on a solution to the problem instead of making excuses for our poor behavior. We only make ourselves feel better with an apology.

HOW TO SAY YOU'RE SORRY

I want you to love your clients. The more you show them love and the more you think about their welfare, the better they'll feel about you and the better you'll feel about you.

When you believe that hearing you say those "magic" apology words will help your client, then yes, say them. Please consider, however, that it was only recently that California enacted a law (yes, a law) allowing a person to apologize at the scene of an accident "without fear of being sandbagged by lawyers exploiting the words as a confession of liability." In e-mail, save your apology for *after* the solution. Take care of your client before you take care of yourself.

Stay focused on the solution to the dilemma you caused for your customer to help her move toward resolution.

When you are writing your apology, keep it real. Prefer the more emotional "I'm sorry" to the more logical "I apologize." After all, if you're in a position where you have to say you're sorry, it is an emotional situation. "I'm sorry" is more authentic, less robotic, and more meaningful than the more polished "apology."

And don't be wishy-washy! Saying something like "I'm sorry about the inconvenience we may have caused you" won't earn any points. If you're in the position of writing an apology, even if you think you didn't do anything wrong, your customer thinks you did. Don't use squirmy words like "*may* have caused you." If you're going to say you're sorry, say it with an authentic heart!

What Not to Say!

Imagine that you are in the hotel or catering business, and you are responsible for the details of a dinner for 1,000 association members. The association executive e-mailed you twice to tell you that the association president (the one who hires and fires the association executive) is allergic to shellfish. You make a note on your banquet event order.

The original agreement specified corn chowder. Somehow, bad pixie dust, or something, got mixed in, and the chef prepares a delicious clam chowder. Because the association president has been assured that everyone knows about his allergy and his dietary restrictions, he doesn't bother to ask the server about the food he is served. While he is talking to the person next to him, he gulps down a tablespoon of clam chowder. He takes a second spoonful and immediately feels his throat begin to swell. The paramedics get to him in time; he spends only one night in the hospital, and he is back at the meeting the next day.

The association executive is more than a little upset with you and demands that you write a letter of apology to the president. Her job is on the line, and she needs you to explain that this is your fault and that she did her due diligence.

Do you need to write a letter of apology or a letter of explanation? Will you begin with an apology? Close with it? Say it twice? Whom will it help? What will you achieve?

Consider your purpose (of course!) by answering the planning questions:

1. *Why?* To ensure that the association executive keeps her job.
2. *What?* Your association executive confirmed multiple times to ensure that no shellfish was served. We should have paid better attention.
3. *Accomplish?* To maintain goodwill; to convince the association president that the association executive did her job and that we will do what it takes to make it right for him.
4. *Next step?* We refund X and offer X.
5. *Delighter?* Your association exec tried everything to ensure a successful meeting.

Dear Mr. Philips:

You never should have had the experience you had at our hotel.

Lois Shirley did everything she could to ensure that all food—from soup to nuts—was cooked with your special dietary needs in mind. She had multiple notes on the BEO and spoke with the chef's assistant at the pre-con. She had every reason to believe that her directive would be followed.

To ease the memory of that evening, the entire meal service for all attendees has been deducted from the final bill. This offers the association a savings of $18,798.

In addition, I would be delighted to host you and a guest for a weekend in the President's Suite. I will make all the arrangements for a delightful weekend for you, including two spa treatments of your choice and a complimentary tee time (for two) on our Golf Digest number one-rated golf course!

```
You will be given VIP treatment from the moment
you arrive. We may not be able to make up for the
miscommunication, but we will try our hardest to
provide you with the service and attention you deserve.

My direct line is 555-555-5555. Please call me
when you are ready for some golf, pampering, and
relaxation. Hope to see you soon.

Sincerely,

Dena Kory
```

If Dena had apologized, where would she have inserted the apology? What and whom would it have helped? What would she have apologized for? The very best thing she could do was what she did: focus on a solution, and on making sure that Lois Shirley didn't have to take any of the blame.

Everything we write has the potential to come back to haunt us. The more you stay focused on what matters to the other person, the more you care about helping her achieve results, the easier it will be for you to move forward to a positive solution and get the results you want.

Be Positive

The last aspect to be considered (or maybe the first!) is to write your message in the most positive, truthful way possible.

Explain the criteria that need to be met, not those that weren't met.

Explain what is possible, not what is impossible.

Explain what you can do or what the other person can have, not what you can't do or what he can't have.

If a client e-mails you requesting five complimentary rooms for every five paid room nights and your policy is one complimentary room for every ten paid room nights, tell him what you can do (one for ten) instead of what you can't. (Stay away from negatives such as that is not possible; our policy doesn't permit; we can't, and so on.)

If you are booked this week or this year and you can't accommodate a client but you are available the day before or the day after, tell her so. Instead of e-mailing, "We are booked on your preferred date," try, "We have availability the day before and the day after your requested date. Will either of these dates work for you?" Tell your reader what is possible and what can happen rather than what can't.

Tell him what you want, not what you don't want.

If you can grant only a 2 percent discount instead of the 20 percent that the client wants, tell the client what you can do. ("We are pleased to offer you a 2 percent courtesy discount. This discount is provided only to our best customers.")

A negative message, effectively written, is no longer negative. It simply is what it is, and the negative connotations are eliminated. By helping your readers understand what is in it for them, or why the situation exists as it does, you help them move forward, and you enjoy the results, recognition, and respect you deserve.

An effective negative sales message—when you can't do what your customer or prospect asks—begins with an educational buffer and helps the reader feel safe and smart continuing to read, then follows with the "bad news" in the most neutral or positive terms possible to help the reader accept the reality. The bad news is followed by additional clarification and an alternative solution (even a delighter when possible) to help the reader accept the situation and take the next step.

When you can't give a customer what she wants, you can still keep her positive and thinking favorably about you and the business relationship. Present what you can do to help the reader create success. Rather than thinking about how you feel and offering an apology, concentrate on how your buyer feels and focus on solving the problem you've created for her. Take the time to plan your message and sales strategy to ensure your message accomplishes what you need it to.

CHAPTER 19

◆ ◆ ◆

HOW TO FOLLOW UP WHEN YOU'RE IGNORED—OR WORSE

The gold is in the follow-up.

—SPEAKERSUE

You've followed all the strategies and tactics in this book, and you still can't get a response from an important prospect. What now? Review your sales writing strategy.

Let's say you wrote an initial "cold" prospecting e-mail to a procurement manager, and it looked like this:

```
Hi Melinda,

Your name was given to me because you are responsible
for procuring the best pricing and highest-quality
products for your company. May I phone you Tuesday to
discuss innovative options to provide ABC with value
and consistently high-quality widgets?
```

Your e-mail was well crafted; you began with a truthful touchpoint, offered a solution, and respectfully asked for an action, the next step, which you supported with the "delighter"— the benefit to Melinda of talking with you. Yet Melinda didn't respond.

You know you need to follow up this introductory e-mail, and the planning process will make your next steps apparent:

1. *Why?* To pique her interest in easily reducing her costs and boosting quality.
2. *What?* When the time is right for you, you may be able to save your company additional money on widget replacement and ordering.
3. *Accomplish?* Help her feel safe and smart talking to me when I call.
4. *Next step?* I call Tuesday morning.
5. *Delighter?* You can feel confident that you're getting the best pricing on the market today and will have an easy time adding us to your preferred vendor list.

Notice the changes in your plan. This time, you'll take the liberty of phoning her rather than waiting for her approval to let you call. In addition, you're aware this might not be the right time for her to pay attention to widget purchases.

Take a few minutes to consider how you would authentically pique your prospect's interest in this follow-up message. What truthful message can you relay?

It's rarely a good idea to begin a follow-up e-mail with: "I'm following up on the e-mail I sent to you last week." Reminding her that you e-mailed her previously will not be likely to motivate her to respond to you. In fact, by doing do, you may annoy her or make her feel that she isn't doing her job well, and that certainly won't endear you to her. This type of opening is weak and about you, the writer.

One of the best things you can do, once you know your purpose, is to put a positive backstory into your own mind regarding your prospect and give her the benefit of the doubt. Instead of thinking that she deliberately ignored your e-mail, replace that thought with something more kindly. Assuming that she most likely never saw your original e-mail because she was so busy or because it went directly into her spam folder will help you write without bias and in a more positive manner.

Your second, or follow-up, e-mail to Melinda might look like this:

```
Subject line: Approved preferred vendor requests
phone call

Hi Melinda,

When the time is right for you, you may be able to
save $$$ on widget replacement and other supplies.
Because ABC has approved preferred vendor status,
adding us as an additional source of widgets for your
location can be quick and easy. I'll call you Tuesday
afternoon to talk about the options available and how
you can count on the best product at the best value.
```

What if she still doesn't respond? I'd phone her again after a reasonable amount of time passes—anywhere between one month and three. I don't want her to think that I'm stalking her by calling any sooner, and I realize that the time may not yet be right for her (because it's about her need for widgets, not my need to make the sale). In my phone call, I would mention that I'll follow up by e-mail so that I have an easy excuse to write to her again. In this attempt, I'd talk about the elephant in the room: that I may be becoming a pest to her.

With the same purpose as the last e-mail in mind, but with the added burden of helping her feel safe and smart talking to me after she has rebuffed me at least three times, my e-mail might say:

```
Subject line: Action request: Monday phone call re
Widgets

Hi Melinda,

At the risk of being a pest, I'm wondering if we can
talk Monday afternoon about widgets that are approved
by your corporate network and can save you up to $
```

```
for each item. Even more important than the reduced
costs may be that ABC widgets are of the highest
quality and have received the L and M guarantee. I'll
phone you Monday so that we can discuss the simple
process of adding ABC to your location's preferred
vendor list. If there is a more convenient time for
you to talk, I'd appreciate it if you would let me
know and I'll follow up as you suggest.
```

And if you still don't hear from her? Start again next quarter. You know you have a high-quality product, and you understand that your selling cycle and your prospect's buying cycle may not be in sync. You also know that circumstances change and that although at present your prospect might be delighted with her current source of widgets, for one reason or another, this may not continue. Review your sales strategy before you write the next e-mail. Remember, your goal is to start a trusting business relationship so that you can get your foot in the door to help your prospect achieve greater success. (I once spent more than three years wooing a prospect. Every time I was scheduled to be in the Chicago area, I e-mailed or called the HR manager asking for a meeting. He responded to my e-mails only twice, once with: "Thank you for your interest, but we currently use the XYZ training company and are pleased with the results." The second response [three years later!] said: "Your perseverance has paid off. The vendor we've been using has recently not met our expectations, and we are currently exploring other options. I'm in the office Friday. Let me know what time you can meet." That was eight years ago, and the amount of time it took me to e-mail, call, e-mail, call, e-mail, call, e-mail, e-mail, call, e-mail, e-mail, e-mail is nothing compared to the revenue I've received.)

WHY GIVING UP IS POINTLESS

When workshop attendees learn that I have 10 different e-mail templates that I personalize for my customers so that I can follow up and counter their resistance, they are often amazed (or think I'm nuts). They are right that not all of the prospects that I pursue turn into loyal clients. But as John Wanamaker famously said, I know "half my advertising is wasted, I just don't know which half."

Here are some tips to ensure that you build your credibility with your prospect and don't annoy him:

1. **Be truthful.** Did you notice the first statement in the third e-mail to Melinda, which said, "At the risk of being a pest"? That is my truth. If my e-mails made it into her inbox and she deleted them, I could certainly be an annoyance to her. My persistence is the elephant in the room, and I want to be the first to bring it up. Additionally, because the point of a prospecting e-mail is to start a likable and trusting relationship, speaking the truth is the best way to accomplish that. Maybe she'll think to herself, "Darn right, you're a pest. I'll never do business with you." Maybe she'll even e-mail me, "I'm not interested. Please do not e-mail me again." If so, she has given me a gift. I'll move on and won't waste her time or mine.

   It is very likely that she might write back, "Thanks. Happy with current vendor. Not interested," in which case I'll do a happy dance. She responded! I now know an objection that I can overcome. The next time I e-mail Melinda, my purpose will be to see if anything has changed (because eventually it always does). Of course, I'll immediately send her an e-mail to respond to her kindness in letting me know where she stands.

```
Subject line: Thank you

Hi Melinda,

Thank you for the update. Because circumstances
sometimes change, I'll plan to follow up with
you early next year to ensure that you're still
receiving great pricing and awesome delivery.

Wishing you all the best.
```

2. **Set yourself apart.** Statistics seem to vary widely regarding how often salespeople follow up and what percentage of them follow up at all. Whether it's 20 percent of salespeople who follow up or 80 percent, however, isn't really important. What is significant is that following up by e-mail is easy, is virtually free, and has the possibility of building a bond between you and your prospect. Develop a follow-up plan that enables you to communicate respectfully on a consistent basis.

3. **Don't make your prospect call you back.** You'll have to work mighty hard to craft an e-mail that is so persuasive and compelling that it motivates a person who doesn't know you, your prospect, to phone you. You need to make it easy for your prospect to do what you want, and a phone call may require too much effort. If you're going to ask him to take the next step, make it as effortless for him as possible ("Please e-mail me with a convenient time for you"; "I'll follow up with you as you suggest"; "As soon as you confirm this . . .").

◆◆◆

The less work your prospect has to do, the better.

You're almost always better served by taking control of the next step ("I'll phone you Wednesday afternoon") and then adding a delighter, a reason for her to accept your call. Don't depend on someone else to be as motivated as you are.

4. **Keep it short.** Try to limit this type of follow-up e-mail to three or four sentences. Your goal isn't to sell the prospect on your product or service; it's to start a trusting relationship and provide enough intrigue about how he might benefit from your product or service that he's willing to accept your next step.

There is another benefit to keeping your prospecting follow-up e-mail brief. If you appear long-winded when you write, the prospect can only assume that you'll blather on the phone, too.

Let him know that you mean business and respect his time by crafting a succinct e-mail selling message.

5. **Vary your approach.** Not every e-mail I sent to the HR manager in Chicago (and current client) was about moving to the next step. You can create rapport and trust by eliminating the "this will benefit you in this way" approach once you've told the prospect that several times. Instead, use your e-mail to send your prospect an article that might help her succeed. Without saying a word about moving to the next step or your product or service, simply e-mail a one-line message ("Hi Name, In case you haven't seen this, I thought it might be interesting to you.") and attach an article you've read or a link to a great blog that will benefit her in her business. The only mention of business is to include your signature line, with your phone number and other contact information.

6. **Don't give up.** Depending on the complexity of the sale, it takes between 7 and 15 contacts to earn the right to the business. If you stop after 4 contacts, you've opened the prospect's eyes, but you haven't brought him to completion. What you've done instead is make it easy for your competition to walk right in, sit right down, and make themselves a deal!

◆◆◆

When you stop following up, it's like you're working on behalf of your competition.

The most important thing to remember about following up is to do it. Do it because you have a product, service, or idea that will help the other person achieve greater success. Do it because you'll stand out and you'll sell more.

PART SIX

◆◆◆

BONUS TO USE RIGHT NOW!

We picked up one excellent word . . . "lagniappe." . . . It is the equivalent of the thirteenth roll in a baker's dozen. It is something thrown in, gratis, for good measure.

—MARK TWAIN

"Would you share your notes with me?" After every workshop, participants e-mail to tell me that they couldn't take notes fast enough and that if I would send them my slide deck, they'd be grateful. So I won't make you ask. Throughout this book, you've read example after example of both excellent and less-than-excellent sales messages. Here you'll find templates that, with personalization for your clients, industry, and sales strategy, you can use immediately.

As you read through these examples, ask yourself: "Does this sound like me? Are these the words I would choose? Is this my truth?"

You may find my writing style and word choice to be too conversational, formal, flippant, serious, wordy, or blunt for your personality and company culture. Follow the patterns and concepts you see here, rather than the exact word choices, so that your message is genuine and compelling.

CHAPTER 20

◆◆◆

WRITING AWESOME
PROSPECTING E-MAILS

*Reinventing the wheel is sometimes the right thing,
when the result is the radial tire.*

—JONATHAN GILBERT

There are times when you should reinvent the wheel and times when you should simply realign it. When the wheel you're driving no longer suits your driving performance needs (or it's flat), it's time for reinvention. These templates I'm about to share with you came about because even just a few years ago, expectations and buying habits were different, and writing styles were different, too. It wasn't unusual for a new hire to be given her predecessor's files and told to copy what was there. If you're still using templates that were passed on to you, it's time to ramp up your performance with these all-season, ultra-high-performance templates!

You've seen variations of some of these e-mails throughout this book, so it should be easy for you to customize and personalize your message with them.

PROSPECTING BASED ON A REFERRAL

A referral is the easiest of all prospecting e-mails to write because it starts with a natural touchpoint. Always start with what you have in common—the referrer. Provide a quick solution to a "pain" you believe the prospect has and explain the next step and why he should be agreeable to accepting or taking it.

> Subject line: Sophie Spaniel suggested I contact you
>
> Hi Name,
>
> Sophie Spaniel told me you're looking for a fun meeting experience for your sales leaders. I'll call you Wednesday morning to talk about how you can rely on our dedicated team of professionals to ensure a fun and memorable event that creates momentum for a successful year of selling.

PROSPECTING THROUGH AN E-LEAD

When your prospect has contacted you through either an e-mail, a Web site lead, or a phone call, you again have an easy touchpoint and a warm e-mail selling message.

> Subject line: Follow up to your request: ABC Meeting—Nov
>
> Hi Name,
>
> You've made a great choice considering XYZ for ABC's annual conference. Attendees feel at home here and the relaxed atmosphere ensures they stay focused and productive.

Based on the information you've provided, I've
attached a preliminary proposal and will call you
later today to ensure that I've covered everything
you need for an outstanding event.

Your attendees will thank you for selecting XYZ!

Here is another situation where you might apply these same skills.
Imagine that you are a dentist specializing in the ABC method. Your
Web site allows potential patients to set up appointment times to consult with you. In the past, more than half of the prospective patients
didn't show up for the appointment time that they themselves had
selected, nor did they answer their phone when your office tried to
call them to confirm. Try this:

Subject line: Confirmation—Consultation scheduled
with Dr. Dentist

Hi Name,

You've come to the right place! You can count on a
perfect smile for a highly professional, confident,
and attractive look.

The consultation with Dr. Dentist is complimentary,
and once you meet her, you'll feel confident about
her advice and techniques. As you requested, I've
scheduled your appointment time for Time, Date. If
you can't make the appointment, you would help me if
you would please call (555-555-5555) or e-mail me so
that we can offer this time to another patient.

Dr. Dentist has helped more than 700 patients in
the past two years, and we are looking forward to
meeting you and welcoming you to the office. You can
count on great results!

PROSPECTING AFTER A TRADE SHOW

You sell promotional products, and you received about 50 cards from prospects at a recent exhibition. You promised each that you would follow up, and you made notes on the back of each business card so that you would easily recall what you talked about when you met that person.

Subject line: Answers to our ABC event discussion: Gifts that enchant!

Hi Name,

Your insights, when we talked at the show last week, were really helpful. Thank you for taking the time to explain what your company needs to accomplish through its use of promotional products.

You mentioned you look for luxury items that are elegant enough for your VIPs to showcase even at home, something beyond the typical cut crystal and sterling silver items they receive from others.

As promised, I've consulted with my colleagues, and we've found several unique gifts that will delight and impress your recipients. I'll phone you tomorrow afternoon to talk about these exclusive products.

Also, in case you haven't seen this article about "What Celebrities Must Have in Their Goody Bag," I thought it might be an enjoyable read for you.

All the best.

FOLLOWING UP A FOLLOW-UP

Even when prospects are interested and have requested information, they may not always respond to your prospecting efforts. Let's say you've sent an e-mail saying that you'll call, and the prospect doesn't take your call. After leaving a pleasant voice mail ("Hi Name, I'm sorry I missed you. I'll follow up with you Date, and if you have a moment, my phone number is 555-555-5555. Thanks so much, and I'm looking forward to helping you impress your sophisticated VIPs with gifts that will enchant them."), your next step is more follow-up.

Following up with customers and prospects offers opportunities to build your business, delight your customers, and keep your sales funnel full.

This next follow-up adds another layer of credibility to the relationship. I might write:

Hi Name,

Wasn't "What Celebrities Must Have in Their Goody Bag" interesting? I was surprised to learn that they prefer practical items! A cashmere sweater that was selected to match the color of their car was more valued than more expensive items because it showed thoughtfulness on the part of the giver. We have lots of creative ideas to show your VIPs how important they are to you. I'll phone you Tuesday morning, and if there is a better time for you, could you let me know? Thanks so much!

PROSPECTING WHEN YOU AND YOUR PROSPECT ARE LINKEDIN, FACEBOOK FRIENDS, OR BELONG TO THE SAME TEMPLE, CHURCH, SORORITY, FRATERNITY, BOWLING TEAM, RUNNING CLUB, OR INDUSTRY GROUP

Because you and your prospective client belong to the same group, you immediately have a bond—a kinship—that can be brought to the forefront of your prospecting efforts. Based on the fact that you and your prospect have this commonality, it's not too forward (or pushy) to ask him for a small favor.

```
Subject line: ABC Association colleague requests
a favor

Hi Name,

As a colleague in the ABC Association, I'm wondering
if I can ask a favor. (This line, of course, might be
changed to say: As a LinkedIn connection, Facebook
Friend, member of Temple Chai, Rah Rah Sorority, the
Runner's Running Club, or whatever, I'm wondering
if I can ask a favor.) May I contact you to learn
more about what is important to you when you are
selecting a destination for your annual meeting/
educational workshops/holiday party? (The slash marks
are here to provide different ideas, not to encourage
you to use them in your e-mail!) We may have a fun
location that is perfect for you, but I want to
be sure I understand your event goals. Would you
have time to talk Wednesday, either by phone or in
person? I'll follow up as you suggest.
```

If the relationship is based on something less mutual, but still in common—for example, if you have a list of parents' names for kids that attend the same school as your son, or you attended a meeting of the

ABC group (but you aren't a member)—your e-mail sales letter will still begin with a genuine touchpoint. If you ask for a favor, however, explain your rationale.

```
Subject line: Follow-up from ABC meeting

Hi Name,

I noticed you are a member of the ABC group, and
I recently attended its networking meeting. Because
Ethan encouraged us to connect after the meeting,
I'm hopeful that it's okay if I ask you a favor.
May I phone you to learn more about your catering
services?

My company provides professional service staff for
home parties, and I'm wondering if there might be a
way for us to work together to serve your clients.
I'll phone you Tuesday morning, but if that isn't a
convenient time for you, I'll be happy to call you
when you suggest.
```

PROSPECTING FROM A PURCHASED LIST

A consulting client asked me to craft what she called "a *true* cold e-mail message." It's possible to do this, I told her, but you always know something about the prospect. Really. You may choose not to use what you know (see the example that follows this one), but by virtue of the prospect's name being on a certain list, you have valuable information to help you "know" the prospect. To determine that authentic commonality, ask yourself: What do the people on this list have in common? What is it that I'm hopeful they are looking for, want, or need?

If you're e-mailing based on a list of people who are responsible for planning meetings, you're contacting them because they plan meetings! That is what you know about them, and it can be enough to provide an authentic touchpoint. What is it that you're hopeful they are looking for, want, or need? To answer this, simply consider what your product or service will do for them. Here is an example:

```
Subject line: Propel sales and inspire creativity

Hello Name,

Your name was given to me because you plan meetings.
If you're looking for an atmosphere that propels
sales and inspires creativity and learning, we may
have a perfect solution for you. (An alternative to
this could be: As a meeting planner, you look for a
learning environment that propels sales and. . . .)

I'll call you Wednesday to learn more about your
meeting objectives and to see if we can help you
accomplish them at great value and in grand fashion.
```

It is possible to write a sales message without any touchpoint, a "true cold e-mail," as my consulting client requested, as long as you rigorously focus on the benefit to the recipient. Here are some options:

```
Subject line: Action request: Call Tuesday morning

Hi Name,

Selecting your next meeting destination may have
just gotten easier. I'll phone you Tuesday morning
to review the exciting, exclusive options ABC is
offering to the XYZ Company.

Subject line: Is your vet trained in the newest
methods to save your pet?
```

Good afternoon Name,

You want your pet to stay by your side as long as possible, yet could you be doing even more to ensure its health? If you have questions about pet care, Dr. Vet is a resource you can trust. A compassionate veterinarian who combines breakthrough medical technology with holistic methods, Dr. Vet does everything possible to ensure a long and happy life for your pet. Please call to schedule an appointment for your pet family members to meet Dr. Vet. Your best friend will have a new friend (and you will too) as soon as they meet!

Subject line: 3 tips to follow after joining a gym

Hello Name,

Congratulations on joining the ABC Gym! You've made a great investment in yourself. Here are 3 tips to help you get the most from your membership:

1. Plan when you'll go. It's too easy to let all the other important things in your life take over your personal time. Schedule when you'll take care of yourself.

2. Always carry your gear in your car. Be ready to pop in and work off that slice of chocolate cake! You can go to the gym for 5 minutes of stress relief or 50 minutes of a cardio burn, but if your gear isn't ready and accessible, it won't happen.

3. Take care of yourself with GoodBars. It's hard to work out if you don't feel like you have any energy. GoodBars are proven to give you the energy lift you need to get through a workout, and more.

Please use this GoodBar coupon so you can taste
how delicious they are. Take GoodBars with you to
the gym today! And if you'd like more workout tips,
I'm here to help!

All the best,

GoodBar Global Sales Rep

Consider your unique selling situation, your purpose and strategy for writing, your company culture, and your personality. Modify each of these prospecting e-mails to ensure that you create templates that work for you again and again, and you'll have no reason to reinvent the wheel each time you write.

CHAPTER 21

◆◆◆

WRITING AMAZING FOLLOW-UP E-MAILS

What simple action could you take today to produce a new momentum toward success in your life?

—ANTHONY ROBBINS

Finding new customers is, of course, an important aspect of selling. Another important way to drive revenue—though for some reason it's not quite as "sexy"—is to delight the customers you currently serve. It's easier, less expensive, and, to my thinking, more satisfying to know that you've engaged clients to such a level that they become raving fans. Not only do delighted customers continue to buy from you, but they also bring new business to you, referring friends and colleagues.

The easiest way of keeping customers happy, beyond providing them with what you say you will, when you say you will, is to stay in touch with them. Your follow-up with your satisfied customers is like money in the bank.

Can you recall the beginning of a romantic relationship? Do you remember how you talked, texted, and titillated each other daily, hourly, or even more often? Then what happened? The hourly phone calls became a.m. and p.m. calls. Then they became once a day—maybe. The sweet notes and cards left became less frequent. The relationship became routine, and although there may have been some comfort in that, one of you may have had the sense of being taken for granted and not appreciated. In fact, when 3,000 unhappily married couples were interviewed and asked, "What is the biggest problem in your marriage?" they didn't cite the usual suspects. They said, "We stopped communicating."

The same thing happens with customers. We woo them. We answer their e-mail messages at all hours, fly cross-country or around the world for the one-hour presentation to their executive team, send tokens of our appreciation, and make them our number one priority. Then what happens? We land the business and, much as in the romantic relationship, we often begin to take them for granted. We're confident that they're getting great service from our outstanding service department and that our product quality is second to none. We begin to let the product talk for us. This mistake is often called "apathy after the sale."

Do your own talking. Use e-mail and other means to communicate, follow up, and love your customers. Beyond showing them the appreciation they deserve, what else happens when you stay in touch with happy clients? You stay fresh in their minds. Your follow-up communications create a relationship, not just a sale.

FOLLOW UP WITH YOUR HAPPY CUSTOMERS TO MAKE THEM HAPPIER

As we discussed throughout this book, your job as a sales professional is to help your buyer feel safe and smart buying from you. By following up after the sale, you accomplish this.

In Scottsdale, we have this wonderful mid-priced Italian chain restaurant that serves a fabulous and unforgettable family-style dinner. We've held our company party there for at least three consecutive years and have enjoyed all sorts of celebrations (my son's fire academy graduation, my birthday, my mom's eighty-fifth birthday) at the restaurant. After most of those occasions, I've gone online to complete the survey expressing delight (and also entering their contest for a $10,000 prize). I never heard back from the restaurant, even though my comments, until this last time, were off-the-charts excellent. I wondered why the restaurant didn't take advantage of my great feedback to reinforce my love affair with its value and taste.

The last time wasn't a positive experience. The product (the food) was fine, but the service delivery was abysmal. I was entertaining three clients, and I was embarrassed that bread wasn't served (although I politely asked for it three times), the appetizers and salads were delivered simultaneously, the preordered vegetarian lasagna was not available, and the "signature" desserts were served with the poorest presentation ever—all squeezed together on one plate as if the restaurant had run out of dishes.

This time when I completed my survey, I immediately received an out-of-office notification from the person in charge of the surveys. Her automated response said that she was gone for two days for a legal holiday, and to please know that she would personally review my comments and get back to me. Good communication.

Three days later, I received a letter in the mail (yes, that kind) thanking me for taking the time to explain my situation. Enclosed were two $25 gift cards. I was impressed both with the amount of service recovery and with the letter sent. I tweeted how excellent the restaurant's follow-up was. Within hours, I received a communication back, thanking me for the tweet and saying how happy the restaurant had been to have the chance to take care of me.

It shouldn't take a negative experience to gain a positive communication, though. By following up with your customers, you create the opportunity to convert more leads into solid business, earn repeat business more easily, and enjoy more frequent referrals and recommendations.

KEEP CUSTOMERS OTHERS LOSE

The single most important thing you can do to be successful today is to communicate with the customers you already have. Make it easy for them to love you.

One of the most strategic times to follow up is immediately after your customer places her first order. Your e-mail can easily prevent buyer's remorse—the little voice in the customer's head that says, "What did I do? Shouldn't I have researched this more or spent the money in a different way?" Your follow-up e-mail calms her fears and quiets the voice by reminding her that she made the right decision. Your words can help her feel safe and smart.

◆ ◆ ◆

The follow-up e-mail doesn't need to be long, just authentic.

Here is an example:

Congratulations! You've made a great choice in selecting E-mail Ninja Kits to help you achieve your sales writing goals. I'll follow up with you next Wednesday to ensure that you're delighted!

Of course, part of follow-up is doing it. If you mention that you'll call or phone or follow up next Wednesday, do it! You might say

As promised, I'm following up with you to ensure that you received the E-mail Ninja Kits last Friday. I'm here to help you, and I've also attached the direct line for each of our support desk managers. You'll be an E-mail Ninja soon!

Or

Thank you for selecting E-mail Ninja Kits for your corporate training program. Your associates will thank you for giving them the tools they need to communicate with today's buyer. Your kits will be delivered by Thursday, and I'm here to help you, if you have questions. Your team will be communicating like E-mail Ninjas very soon!

Or

What a great choice you made selecting ABC for your upcoming meeting! From the moment your guests arrive, they'll know how much you appreciate their hard work during this challenging year. Count on them leaving here energized and ready to sell more so that they can participate in next year's incentive trip, too!

Or

You can count on a productive and fun meeting at ABC! An event manager will call you next week to start the official planning process to ensure that your meeting meets your expectations in every way. If you have any questions, I am here to help, though I know you'll be in great hands with our dedicated and experienced event management team.

Thanks again for choosing ABC. We look forward to warmly welcoming you soon.

At what other times is it important that you follow up with your delighted customers? Follow-up should be consistent and planned. Depending on the nature of the sale and the business, you might want to e-mail again 30 days after the sale is complete or delivered, and then again at 90 days. After that, find a reason to stay in touch at least once a quarter. If that strategy is totally unrealistic for you (could it be that you're too busy drumming up new business because your existing customers go elsewhere?), e-mail your customers at least every six months.

FOLLOW UP AT HOLIDAYS, SINCERELY

Holiday greetings count as follow-up and are appreciated as long as they are from you, not your marketing department's attempt to convey good feelings with a sterile PDF and a generic greeting. (That type of greeting doesn't count as a follow-up communication because it isn't; it's marketing!) E-mail a personal message by mentioning something about your relationship that will help the other person feel good about himself or about your relationship with him. Write about an accomplishment of his that impacted his company, or something that touches him and reminds him that you have a successful relationship.

Remember, the purpose of the follow-up e-mail isn't always to ask for future business. Sometimes it's simply to help the client feel appreciated, which, of course, helps you stay fresh in her mind. Pretending to send a thank you or a holiday greeting when what you're really sending is a sales piece is disingenuous and will be ineffective.

Other times to follow up include whenever you have information that will help the client—relevant content such as new products, new pricing, new schedules, new menus, or new anything. Additionally, when you come across a white paper or a blog post—anything you think he'll enjoy reading (that is appropriate and professional)—e-mail it to him with a quick message: "Hi Name, I thought you might enjoy reading about the 'spaghetti bowl concept.' I never knew that what we were talking about had a name!"

Another way to follow up is to "like" them on Facebook and link to them on LinkedIn. Every time you interact, it counts as a follow-up message. By commenting on their company's fan page or on the client's personal page in a professional, strategic manner, you can reduce the number of business e-mails you send. When you post comments on the site, remember why you're doing it—to connect with the client. All public comments should be written as professional-sounding business messages.

Always communicate to build bridges, not to burn them.

The more opportunities you take to show your customers that they're top-of-mind for you, the more likely it is that you'll be top-of-mind for them.

CHAPTER 22

◆◆◆

ENHANCE YOUR WORTH

Have no fear of perfection—you'll never reach it.
—SALVADOR DALI

At first, Dali's words struck me as incredibly sad. How dismal life would be if we never thought that we had a glimmer of hope of achieving perfection. The more I thought about his words, though, the more liberating they became to me. The reality is that we can't reach perfection. We can only do the best we can, and that is enough.

Once we give up trying to do things perfectly, we can enjoy doing them. And even though we may not be able to do things perfectly, we can do them better—much better—than we're doing them now.

We can get better results, we can help more people, and we can lead a more productive and successful life. That is what this book has been about. We can enjoy greater respect and recognition for our ideas and get better results every time we communicate.

Here are some ideas to think about:

- **Know your purpose for writing.** You can't get where you want to go if you don't know where you want to go.
- **Format your message for maximum impact.** Help your readers feel safe and smart. Answer their unasked questions. Begin with

a touchpoint. Be concise. Use simple, crisp, clear words. People need lots of motivation to read and act upon a sales letter.

- **Focus on the reader and what is important to him.** Regardless of what you have to offer and how spectacular it may be, if your prospects don't see what is in it for them, you won't connect, you won't have an impact, and you won't sell. From their perspective, in their shoes, from their heart, what matters? Offer them the solutions to their problems, challenges, and heartaches, and they'll close the deal for you. Become your customer.

- **Present your message in the most positive light possible.** People like hearing about what they can do, not what they can't do. They want to know what criteria have been met, not what haven't been. Reframe your messages to be as pleasant and as likable as is reasonable. Not only will this change other people's outlook about your message, it may even change your own.

- **Words make a difference.** Write your message, even a quick e-mail, so that if it appears in the company newsletter, people will respect you for it. Every communication should sell your positive reputation.

- **Bother with correct grammar and punctuation.** Many of your readers won't care, but those who do will value you and your abilities more than you can imagine.

- **Use conversational language.** Avoid using the thesaurus to make yourself look good. You are good already. Write your message the way you would say it. Stephen King said, "Any word you have to hunt for in a thesaurus is the wrong word. There are no exceptions to this rule." Depend on words you're comfortable with and are certain to mean what you intend.

- **Honor your recipient by taking the time to reread your e-mail before sending it.** Good writers use the third step in the writing process (checking) to catch anything that might not be in the best taste or be the most appropriate phrase.

- **Follow up.** Jay Conrad Levinson, in his book *Guerrilla Marketing*, suggests that the main reason sales are lost is not poor quality or rotten service. He says that apathy after the sale is the primary reason that businesses lose customers. Levinson writes, "A numbing 68% of all business lost . . . is lost due to apathy after the sale." If a relationship is to grow, it needs to be tended. Communicate. Communicate. Communicate!

When you take the time to make your customers feel appreciated, when they know that you are grateful for their business and the opportunity to serve them, and when you take a moment to remind them that they selected the best, can expect the best, and will receive the best, you transcend buyer's remorse. Now they're doing business with a trusted partner, not with someone who simply wants the business.

The lyrics to an old Shirelles song asked, "Will you still love me tomorrow?" Your customers and your colleagues wonder the same thing. The very best way to solidify any relationship is to show true appreciation for that relationship.

- **Write thank you notes.** They take very little time and mean so much to the receiver. Be as specific as possible about what you are thanking the person for. ("I appreciate how quickly you got me the answers to my questions. You made me look good. Thanks so much.") Jim Rohn said, "Kind words can be short and easy to speak, but their echoes are truly endless."
- **Use the templates, your way.** Create templates you can personalize for your customers, using your voice and your company culture. There is no need to start writing from scratch every time when you have a strong base.
- **Make a list of the 10 most important ideas you discovered in this book.** Select the two most important of those ideas and write them on a sticky note and stick it on your computer. Use those ideas. Concentrate on applying only those two new ideas. By the end of the month, you'll own those techniques. They'll be new habits that you won't even have to think about using. Next month, select two more to implement. The month after that, choose two more.

Watch your sales and profits soar and your professionalism dramatically improve. You'll feel confident about using your new sales tool—the written word—as you reap huge dividends in respect, recognition, and results.

Thank you for reading this book, and please remember what Thomas Edison said: "The value of an idea lies in the using of it."

INDEX

ABOUT THE AUTHOR

Sue Hershkowitz-Coore is the author of *Power Sales Writing* and *How to Say It to Sell It*. She lives with her husband, Bill, and their two dogs, Sophie and BC, in Scottsdale, Arizona.

Known as "SpeakerSue," Sue has been compared to Rita Rudner, the Energizer Bunny™, and Red Bull (but better for you). She is available for consultation, corporate and association speaking engagements, and sales training workshops. She provides a variety of blended learning solutions to help your team convert leads into booked business and enhance its professionalism, profits, and productivity.

Sue can be contacted through her Web site, www.SpeakerSue.com, reached by e-mail at Sue@SpeakerSue.com, or by phoning her U.S. office at +1 480-575-9711. For a complimentary download of the five planning questions and other free tools, click on the Free Stuff tab on her Web site. Use the promo code SellMore where requested.

You can follow SpeakerSue on Twitter (http://twitter.com/SpeakerSue) and Facebook, and receive tips to improve sales writing six times a year by registering at the Web site for SpeakerSueSays, her complimentary e-zine.